GROWING UP
COLT

A Father, a Son,
a Life in Football

COLT McCOY
& BRAD McCOY
WITH MIKE YORKEY

BARBOUR
PUBLISHING

© 2011 by Koyboys LLC

ISBN 978-1-61626-659-2

All rights reserved. No part of this publication may be reproduced or transmitted for commercial purposes, except for brief quotations in printed reviews, without written permission of the publisher.

Churches and other noncommercial interests may reproduce portions of this book without the express written permission of Barbour Publishing, provided that the text does not exceed 500 words and that the text is not material quoted from another publisher. When reproducing text from this book, include the following credit line: "From *Growing Up Colt*, published by Barbour Publishing, Inc. Used by permission."

Scripture taken from the HOLY BIBLE, NEW INTERNATIONAL VERSION®. NIV®. Copyright © 1973, 1978, 1984, 2010 by Biblica, Inc.™ Used by permission. All rights reserved worldwide.

Scripture quotation marked TLB is taken from The Living Bible © 1971. Used by permission of Tyndale House Publishers, Inc. Wheaton, Illinois 60189. All rights reserved.

Cover, back, and author photographs: Trevor Gerland Productions

Colt McCoy is represented by The Agency Sports Management LLC, 230 Park Avenue, Suite 851, New York, New York 10169.

Mike Yorkey is represented by WordServe Literary Group, Ltd., Greg Johnson, Literary Agent, 10152 S. Knoll Circle, Highlands Ranch, CO 80130

Published by Barbour Publishing, Inc., P.O. Box 719, Uhrichsville, Ohio 44683 www.barbourbooks.com

Our mission is to publish and distribute inspirational products offering exceptional value and biblical encouragement to the masses.

ecpa Member of the
Evangelical Christian
Publishers Association

Printed in the United States of America.

Contents

FOREWORD

I've always had an open-door policy as far as players are concerned, so it isn't uncommon for one to drop by with something on his mind. It didn't shock me one day when my assistant Kasey Johnson said our redshirt freshman quarterback Colt McCoy wanted to see me.

It was what happened next that surprised me.

A season before, we had won the BCS Championship Game against Southern Cal in the Rose Bowl. Vince Young, our quarterback, had led us to two straight Rose Bowl victories. But after the USC game, Vince decided to jump to the NFL. As we approached our 2006 spring training, we needed a new leader.

Colt had been a true freshman on that national championship team. But since we had chosen to redshirt him (by not playing that season, he saved a year of eligibility) he had worked only in practice, watching every snap Vince took.

That spring, Colt fought a spirited battle for the starting quarterback spot with a young man named Jevan Snead, who had entered college early after a sensational high school career. Spring practice ended with the two about even, and we knew their individual work through the summer and fall training (beginning in August) would determine our starter. We didn't have much time to prepare—our second game would be against No. 1-ranked Ohio State.

When Colt arrived, I knew from his look that he had something on his mind. There was determination in his eyes, even if he was a little nervous entering his head coach's office.

Before I could say "hello," Colt blurted out: "I'm going to be your quarterback, and I'm going to lead us to the national championship."

Then he turned and walked out the door.

When fall practice ended, Colt had earned the job—and the rest, as they say, is history. We lost only one game a year in 2008 and 2009, finishing third and second nationally. Colt won more games as a starting quarterback than anyone in NCAA history. His senior year, we won the Big 12 Championship, and—true to his word—he took us to the BCS Championship game in Pasadena. Of the eight games we lost in Colt's four years as starter, one was when the other team scored with one second left. In three losses—including that national championship game—he'd had to leave because of injury.

Colt's story begins in the small towns of Texas, where "Friday Night Lights" are part of the fiber of the community. It's a story of a family with its values in the right order: faith, family, and football.

Colt's passion for the game is matched only by his commitment to his faith, which together drive his will to win and his determination never to give up. As a 170-pounder from a small high school, he might have been happy just to be at a school like Texas—but not Colt. In this book, you'll learn of his work in the weight room, his continued growth in understanding of the game, and his grasp of the responsibility of a star athlete to be a role model. That sort of success comes from his roots.

Today, Colt and his wife, Rachel, have become friends, special people in our lives. They touch everyone with their love for each other and their compassion for people and the world around them.

Some folks come into your life, pass through, and move on. Colt McCoy is one who stays with you forever—not for what he's done, but for who he is.

MACK BROWN
HEAD FOOTBALL COACH
THE UNIVERSITY OF TEXAS LONGHORNS

A Note to the Reader
by Colt McCoy

Less than a week after I played in my final collegiate football game for the University of Texas in the 2010 Bowl Championship Series Championship Game, my father, Brad McCoy, fulfilled a commitment he had made months earlier to speak at the Regents School of Austin's annual sports banquet.

Dad, who'd been a high school football coach for twenty-seven years, had been asked to speak about growing leaders and the importance of sports, especially football, in teaching life's lessons. He prefaced his keynote speech by stating he would be talking about four principles that he and my mom, Debra, employed while raising me and my two younger brothers. Very quickly, they were:

1. Prepare your children for the path, not the path for your children. My father said he and Mom followed the godly advice in Proverbs 22:6, which goes like this: "Start children off on the way they should go, and even when they are old they will not turn from it."

All too often, Dad said, he saw parents seeking to smooth out life's bumps in the road for their children. If these "bulldozer parents" weren't in his coach's office demanding to know why Johnny wasn't playing, they were letting their kids slide by at home because they didn't want to be too "tough" on them. Every parent, Dad reminded the audience, must teach his or her children how to work hard and study hard, the discipline of setting goals and attaining them, the resilience of getting back on their feet when life knocks them down, and the value of never giving up.

Preparing children for the path means not being afraid to discipline children when they fall out of line or show willful disobedience. Many parents, Dad said, do not punish their children because they fear not being liked by their offspring, but withholding discipline can do more harm to a child's future.

2. Prepare your children to do their best. Success in any endeavor—from academics to sports to life itself—starts with teaching children what it means to set a goal and to work hard to achieve it. Children need high expectations so they will learn what it takes to do their best. As a high school coach for most of his adult life, my father would lead his teams onto the field with the chant, "Expect to win, play to win!" Children need to hear the same high expectations from their parents.

3. Prepare your children to be leaders. Besides striving to do their best, children should be taught how to lead as well, and that means teaching children to look for ways to serve others and inspire those around them. Dad taught me the biblical truth that if I wanted to be a leader, I had to be a servant first.

4. Prepare your children for open and closed doors. This is where my father became emotional during his talk at Regents School. He said his emotions were still raw after what happened to me at the BCS Championship Game against the University of Alabama a few days earlier. On our fifth offensive play from scrimmage, a 296-pound University of Alabama defensive lineman, Marcell Dareus, hit me with a pretty good shot.

Dad said he had seen me take a ton of big hits during my four seasons playing quarterback at Texas, but he immediately knew something was wrong when I got up from the pile and began jogging off the field, rotating my right shoulder and motioning with my left arm for someone to replace me.

I would never play another down of college football for the

University of Texas, but what hurt more than my bum shoulder, my father said, was that I couldn't help my team win the BCS national championship. Everything I had worked for up to then—everything that I had built upon—was gone in an instant. In the biggest game of my collegiate career, and at a time when my team needed me the most, all I could do was stand on the sidelines and watch.

"When Colt's dreams of playing for the national title were dashed, God closed a door," Dad said. "But that didn't mean that God didn't have a plan or open a different door." (My father and I will have a lot more to say about what happened at the 2010 BCS Championship Game in chapter 13.)

Well, unbeknownst to Dad, someone in the audience was taking notes that night and wrote a blog about my father's "amazing" message. This father recapped the four points as well as some of the other things Dad shared.

Don't ask me how or why this happened, but word of Dad's talk went "viral," as people forwarded the link or copied and pasted Dad's talk in e-mails and passed it along in cyberspace. Dad's talk took on a life of its own, and suddenly everyone and their cousins were sending the link to their friends, who passed it along to their friends . . . .

As a result, Dad received tons of speaking requests, along with appeals that I join him to talk about what I had learned growing up. We accepted as many speaking engagements as we could, although I was busy in 2010 preparing for the NFL draft, moving to Cleveland to start my professional career, and getting married to the former Rachel Glandorf during the summer. Since we couldn't keep up with the requests to share our stories and life experiences in person, my father and I decided to write *Growing Up Colt*.

I'm aware that most NFL quarterbacks—if they ever do write a book—usually do so after winning a Super Bowl or retiring following a Hall of Fame career. I'll be twenty-five years old when the 2011 NFL season starts, so in a way my professional football career is ahead of me.

Throughout my life so far, I've put in a lot of hard work, and I'll have to keep working hard to succeed in the NFL. I've tried to do my best—one of the four Bible-based principles Dad raised me with—and though I haven't been perfect, I'm proud of the way my parents brought me up. As you'll see in this book, I wouldn't be where I am today without their valuable input and hands-on parental guidance.

Not only will you learn how Dad's principles shaped me and my character, but I think you'll enjoy some stories about my time in a small Texas high school, at the highest levels of college football at the University of Texas, and in the NFL with the Cleveland Browns.

But don't get the idea that Dad and Mom are "football parents" who micromanaged my life every step of the way and can't let go even though I'm married and playing in the NFL. Instead, they always said their goal was to work their way out of a job by training me to be a leader and to serve others.

As you'll see in *Growing Up Colt*, I'm the beneficiary of the great foundation they laid down.

CHAPTER 1

Rookie Start
in Blitzburgh

Colt McCoy

The distance between the Cleveland Browns Training Complex in Berea, Ohio, and downtown Pittsburgh is only 135 miles, a journey of two and a half hours.

As our chartered caravan of Cleveland Browns buses rolled through the Ohio countryside one balmy mid-October afternoon, I barely glanced at the crimson-and-gold fall foliage outside my window. Instead, I paid close attention to what our offensive coordinator, Brian Daboll, was saying about the intricacies of the Browns' offense as well as the tendencies of the Pittsburgh Steelers' defense.

I had been cramming all week for my first start as an NFL quarterback. I listened intently to Coach Daboll as he flipped through the Browns' playbook. Nothing inside the thick volume was new to me. All fall long, I had prepared myself like I was the starting quarterback, even though I had been relegated to the bench as a third-stringer. That meant reviewing the playbook and the terminology, studying film, working out in the weight room, and paying attention in team meetings.

It didn't mean practicing with the first or second team, however. Since the end of preseason, I had stood on the sidelines and watched our starting quarterback, Jake Delhomme, take snaps from center and work on our plays. Our No. 2 quarterback, Seneca Wallace, called signals for the scout team that practiced against our defense. All I could do was stand on the sidelines, toss a

11

In our 2010 season opener, Jake twisted his ankle but kept playing against the Tampa Bay Buccaneers, a game we lost by a field goal, 17–14. When Seneca Wallace moved into the starting lineup, I was still treated like the third quarterback on the depth chart. Even though I ached to contribute to my team, I was the forgotten man on the roster. Coming from the University of Texas—where I had started fifty-three consecutive games over four seasons—I was used to playing, to being *the guy.* It was tough not getting to play, but I knew I had to be patient.

Just before halftime against the Atlanta Falcons in Week 4, Seneca took a big hit on a sack and went down. We had to take a timeout so the trainers could assist him back to the bench. The way he was limping, it looked like another ankle injury.

We were running out of quarterbacks. I edged closer to our head coach, Eric Mangini, secretly hoping he'd say, "It's your turn, Colt. Get in there." But Coach Mangini never looked my way. Instead, he found Jake Delhomme and asked him if he could get back in the game.

Everyone knew Jake's ankle wasn't ready, but Coach Mangini sent him back on the field to play anyway. That sent a signal loud and clear that Coach was doing everything he could to *not* give me the ball.

Jake found his helmet, took the field, and tossed a short pass to end the first half, and we jogged off the field at Cleveland Browns Stadium nursing a 7–6 lead against the Falcons, who came into town with a 3–1 record. (The Falcons were a good team on their way to an NFC–leading 13–3 record.)

There was no talk in the locker room of bringing me in, however, so all I could do was pace the sidelines as play resumed after intermission. During the second half, though, Jake reinjured his right ankle in a sack. Jake hobbled between plays, but he gritted his teeth and hung in there. The game was decided with about five minutes left. We were down 13–7 but driving the ball. The Falcons intercepted Jake's short pass and ran it back for a touchdown, ending our hopes. The frustrating loss dropped our record to 1–4, and it looked like the Browns were heading toward another dismal season.

The following day, a Monday, I drove to the Cleveland Browns training facility, wondering what would happen next. The Browns were down to one healthy quarterback—me. Since the Cleveland coaches had treated me like a leper since the season began, I figured they were busy making phone calls to bring in a veteran free agent.

Ever since I reported to training camp, I had gotten the message loud and clear: *Colt, you're not going to play this year. Your job is to watch and listen.* When I walked into the Browns' headquarters that morning, however, I was greeted like a long-lost family member who had unexpectedly shown up at a McCoy summer reunion. The slaps on the back and cries of "How ya doing, Colt?" were followed by "Coach wants to see you."

I marched into Coach Mangini's office, and he warmly greeted me and offered me a chair. "Colt, we need to get you ready for this weekend against Pittsburgh. You're starting."

I smiled. Just like that, I had gone from third-stringer to starting quarterback. My heart raced with excitement. I had been seriously itching to play all season long, and now I would get my chance to play in an NFL game and fulfill my boyhood dream.

At the same time, though, I knew all too well *who* we were playing that Sunday—the Pittsburgh Steelers—and *where*—on their home turf, Heinz Field. Visions of sixty-five thousand swirling Terrible Towels came into my mind, as well as stories

I'd heard about how brutal the Steelers fans were on opposing teams, especially untested quarterbacks.

Nothing like being thrown to the wolves the first time out.

When I called my dad with the news, the first thing he said was, "Congratulations, son. That's awesome!"

"Yeah, it's awesome, and I'm going to be fired up," I replied. "I wouldn't have it any other way. I get to play the Steelers, our division rivals, on the road for my first start. If I can go out there and play against *their* defense, I can play against anybody in the league."

I knew Pittsburgh had the No. 1 defense in the NFL and that their linebackers attacked the quarterback so often that people called them "Blitzburgh." But I saw nothing but opportunity.

"That's great to hear," my father said. "There's no other team that you'd want to start against because you're going to be gauged by how you play against the best."

Now our team buses were heading into Steelers territory as we crossed the Allegheny River into downtown Pittsburgh. We were a dispirited bunch after losing so many close games, and it looked like our season would get even darker following the Atlanta loss. Looming ahead was a murderer's row of elite NFL teams: after taking on Pittsburgh, we would face the New Orleans Saints, the New England Patriots, and the New York Jets—all top-tier franchises bound for the 2010 NFL playoffs.

Coach Daboll looked down at this notes. "Keep an eye on Polamalu. When he lines up strong side, and the free safety is in the middle of the field, expect him to blitz off the edge."

Coach was talking about Troy Polamalu, whose mane of thick, curly, black hair stuck out of his helmet and ran halfway down his back. Many of the football pundits on ESPN and on the NFL pregame shows believed Polamalu was the best defensive player in the league, and they certainly had plenty of highlights to draw from to make their case. Number 43 seemed to be everywhere on *and* off the field, thanks to his playmaking abilities and his advertisements for Head & Shoulders shampoo shown during televised games.

Polamalu and the rest of the Pittsburgh defense were known as the "Steel Curtain" around the league. (That nickname started in the 1970s and stuck through the years.) The Steelers' defensive backs were celebrated for pummeling quarterbacks and delivering vicious hits on receivers. But Polamalu wasn't the only defensive star playing in Pittsburgh. Coach reminded me to look out for another linebacker: James Harrison, who was bigger and bulkier than Polamalu and thus more lethal. When No. 92 got in a shot, quarterbacks sometimes didn't get up.

We pulled up to the Westin Convention Center hotel just as darkness fell on Pittsburgh. The plan was for us to check into our rooms and then report for dinner, followed by a team meeting in one of the hotel conference rooms.

The team meeting on the eve of a football game was our last chance to go through that week's game plan. The coaching staff would review how we were going to attack the Pittsburgh defense as well as defend against a powerful Steelers offense led by quarterback Ben Roethlisberger, one of the best quarterbacks in the league and a proven winner, as evidenced by the two Super Bowl rings on his fingers.

As if we didn't have our hands full already, we would also have to contend with the emotional return of "Big Ben"—as the media called him—to NFL football. Commissioner Roger Goodell had suspended Roethlisberger for six games for violating the NFL's personal conduct policy after Ben was accused of sexual assault during the off-season. Goodell later reduced the suspension to four games after the contrite quarterback submitted to counseling and extensive evaluations.

Playing as if they wanted to prove to the league that they could weather the storm without their star quarterback under center, the Steelers had won three of their four games without Big Ben. Now that Roethlisberger was returning to the team, everyone in the Browns' team meeting sensed that the Steelers would be sky high, spurred on by their fans going crazy when their prodigal son stepped onto the field.

At Saturday night team meetings earlier in the season, Coach Mangini always had guys stand up and say something inspirational or talk about how they felt. For instance, if a guy on our team used to play for that week's opponent, Coach would ask him to describe what this game meant to him or what we needed to do to win the next day.

This would be my first NFL start, and something in my gut told me that I should say something to my teammates. I knew they had questions about me swirling in their minds: *How are we going to play the Steelers—one of the best teams in the league—with a rookie quarterback who's never taken a snap at this level? What chance do we have to win—in Pittsburgh of all places?*

After the team dinner, I approached Coach Mangini and told him, "I know you're going to call on me. I'll be ready."

He just smiled. *Whatever.*

When the time came for Coach to call on players to speak, he turned to me first and announced that I had something to say. Rising to my feet, I stood next to my table and looked around the conference room at my fifty-three teammates, a half-dozen players who wouldn't be suiting up in the morning, and our coaching staff and team officials.

"I want you guys to know that I haven't embraced being the third-string quarterback," I began. "I love and respect Jake and Seneca, but now that they're hurt, it's my turn to step in here and play.

"I know you have no idea what it's going to be like tomorrow. Everyone in here is scared stiff about a rookie going into Pittsburgh and having his first start. If you want to be scared, be scared. I'm not scared. I'm ready to play. I'm excited. I'm fired up. This is my passion. This is what I love to do. And I can't wait to get out there and play with all you guys tomorrow.

"Our game tomorrow is going to be the start of something great. Bring your all because I know I'm bringing all mine. The hay is in the barn. Let's go."

Let's just say that I saw a lot of big eyes and stunned faces looking back at me. You could have run a herd of Texas longhorns—real ones—through that conference room and no one would have noticed. But those surprised looks quickly changed to smiles, followed by a few chuckles, after my "hay is in the barn" line.

Actually, that was the second time in two days that some of my teammates had heard me use the phrase. At our practice the day before, I ended our workout by gathering the offense around me. It's called a "breakdown" in football, and usually what happens is that all the players gather in a circle around the quarterback, who does a final "fire up" before everyone breaks to take a shower.

Often, quarterbacks scream something like, "Win on three . . . one, two, three—"

"Win!" everyone yells.

But for my first breakdown, I wanted to do something different.

"The hay's in the barn," I announced in a loud voice. "Let's go win this thing. Win on three . . . one, two, three—"

"Win!" my teammates yelled.

But nobody left for the locker room.

"The hay's in the barn?" asked one of my wide receivers. "Dude, what does that mean?"

The rest of the offense had quizzical looks on their faces, too.

Time for an agricultural tutorial.

"Look, where I come from, you have a harvest season," I said. "You plant the hay grazer, you let it grow, you watch it grow, you cut it, you bale it, and you put the bales on the trailer. You drive the trailer around and park it and put the hay in the barn. When all the hay is out of the field and in the barn, your work is done and you're ready for the next thing."

I had everyone's attention now.

"That's what this week is. We worked, we worked, and we worked. I worked, I worked, and I worked. The hay is in the barn, man. It's Friday. No more practice. Now it's time to go win. Our work is done."

"That's cool, Colt," said one of my teammates.

"Okay," said another. "I get it now."

When our team meeting was over, I headed up to my room. After taking a shower, I immediately fell asleep with no anxiety whatsoever. That's the way it's always been for me on the night before a game. I slept hard because I knew my preparation was done.

The hay was in the barn.

Brad McCoy

While Colt was turning in for the evening, my wife, Debra, and I checked into our room at the Omni William Penn Hotel. We had flown in from Lincoln, Nebraska, with our good friend Dick Anderson. That afternoon, the three of us had watched the University of Texas upset the fifth-ranked Nebraska Cornhuskers 20–13. Dick was a Nebraska fan, even though he lived in Austin, home of the University of Texas. (Dick was also Colt's landlord for two years, but more on that story later.)

We had made the trek to Lincoln because our youngest son, Case, was the second-string quarterback at Texas. He had won the backup position as a true freshman, meaning that for the sixth consecutive year, a McCoy quarterback was suiting up for UT. After losses to UCLA and Oklahoma, the Longhorns weren't expected to beat Nebraska on the road, but Coach Mack Brown's team stunned the college football world with a huge, surprising victory.

Five hours later, we found ourselves in Pittsburgh, terribly excited but also terribly anxious about Colt's first NFL start. Colt's wife, Rachel, had driven in from Cleveland with a college friend, Leslie Peterson, and they were staying in Pittsburgh with a friend Rachel knew from Baylor University, where she attended college. We were thankful they had arrived safely, and we made arrangements to meet up with Rachel and her friend in the morning.

Debra and I awoke just after dawn, which is our custom. We began our day by bowing our heads and praying for Colt's safety and protection. After our prayer time, I could tell Debra was a bit keyed up and nervous. She's been a coach's wife for many years and had watched her three sons play in hundreds of games over the years, but I could sense her apprehension. That was certainly understandable. There's always a certain amount of fear in every mother's heart when her son straps on a helmet and jogs onto the field—even more so this time because this was the NFL.

Debra is a student of the game, and she knew that the kind of football played in the NFL was a quantum leap from Division I college. The size, speed, and intensity of NFL players brought a whole new meaning to the nerves she felt that morning. I felt the butterflies in my stomach as well, but also a full helping of fatherly pride. My son—my offspring whom I had brought up from nothing—was fixing to start an NFL regular season game against the Pittsburgh Steelers, who many thought were the best team in pro football. My son would be playing quarterback, the premier position in football—maybe all of sports—before more than sixty-five thousand rabid Steelers fans and millions of TV viewers. How cool was that?

I reached for my cell phone and dialed Colt's number. I knew he wouldn't pick up because he always turned off his iPhone the night before the game. But he and I had a pregame ritual we had started his first season at the University of Texas: me calling him on the morning of game day.

"Colt, this is Dad. This is your weekly good luck call. I want to encourage you to do your best today. We've been through this for a long time, and you know how much your family loves you. You're going to do great today. Don't get your head down if you make a mistake. Come back, fight hard, and be a leader. Keep your feet moving and your eyes up, and we'll see you after the game. I love you, Son, and I'm proud of you."

I hung up, knowing that Colt wouldn't listen to the message until after the game. So why did I call? Because it was our father-son tradition, and I knew he'd notice if I *didn't* call. That happened one time: when he was playing in a college game at Iowa State. I had hitched a ride on a private plane to Ames, Iowa, on the morning of the game. En route, we ran into thunderstorm problems and had to turn around. By the time we touched down in Dallas, it was too late to call Colt.

That evening, Colt wondered where his pregame call was. "I knew something must have happened," he said after learning why I couldn't call.

Debra and I took the glass elevator down to the lobby, where we met up with Dick, Rachel, and Leslie. We mutually decided that Dick and I would make a pilgrimage to Jerome Bettis' Grille 36 for an early lunch while Debra and the girls took off to explore the city—and find a Starbucks. Debra loved her tall coffee with whip and the Perfect Oatmeal with toppings of dried fruit and mixed nuts. Armed with cell phones, we made arrangements to meet at Heinz Field.

Dick and I walked around downtown Pittsburgh before finding Grille 36. Voted the best sports restaurant in Pittsburgh, Jerome Bettis' Grille 36 was owned by the retired Steelers running back nicknamed "The Bus." The shiny restaurant, which had plenty of flat-screen TVs hanging from the ceiling, was located between Heinz Field and PNC Park, where the Pittsburgh Pirates played major league baseball.

The Bus' place was always packed on game day. It looked like several hundred Steelers fans were jammed inside the restaurant that day, many of them standing around the gleaming bars with adult beverages in their hands. The noise was deafening, and Dick and I could barely hear each other talk in between bites of our burgers and fries.

Colt

I knew Rachel and my parents were in Pittsburgh for my first NFL start, but I wasn't thinking about what they could be doing. It was Sunday morning, and I had my game face on. I tried to minimize all distractions.

Our team buses left the hotel and headed toward the stadium. As we pulled up to Heinz Field, I got my first glimpse from behind my darkly tinted window of just how *serious* the Steelers fans can be. A couple of thousand fans—standing shoulder to shoulder and six or seven deep—raised quite a ruckus as our caravan approached under police escort. Most were yelling stuff that would have earned me a washing-my-mouth-with-soap episode if I had said them in my mother's presence when I was a kid. Burly guys wearing Roethlisberger jerseys wadded up balls of trash and threw them in our direction, but most didn't have Big Ben's good aim. The occasional beer bottle or aluminum can struck our bus, and gray-haired grandmas flipped us the bird.

The only time I'd witnessed a similar scene was when I was in college and we were bused to the Cotton Bowl in downtown Dallas for the Red River Rivalry game between Texas and Oklahoma. Sooners fans exhibited crude behavior and took great delight in yelling obscene chants.

I was surprised how calm I felt—or maybe I should say how calm I felt given the circumstances. I well understood the game's implications for my future as well as the microscope I was under. Mentally, I felt ready to play because I had studied the quarterback position so hard since my first minicamp. Physically, however, I hadn't gotten the "reps"—the repetitions—with our offense all season long, so I knew I would be playing catch-up.

If I was going to play well against the Steelers, then I'd have to adjust to something called "NFL game speed" right from the first snap.

Brad

Dick and I wanted to get to the stadium good and early so we could take in the NFL pregame atmosphere. We didn't live close to Dallas, so I hadn't attended too many professional games over the years, but we were big fans of "America's Team," the Dallas Cowboys. One of Colt's favorite players growing up was Cowboy quarterback Troy Aikman.

We had learned just a few days earlier that Colt would be starting, so we had to scramble for tickets. Colt said the few seats allotted to the Browns organization weren't very good, so I made a phone call to the Pittsburgh Steelers front office and explained my situation. They were very accommodating and sold us four excellent field level seats located at the 45-yard line, about twenty rows up. Dick's seat was in another section.

We reached our seats about an hour before game time, just as both teams came onto the field to warm up. My eyes trained on Colt, who was wearing a white No. 12 jersey—the same number he wore at Texas—as he loosened up. I have to admit that the whole scene was surreal. As I watched my son in an NFL uniform making warm-up tosses to his receivers, I thought how he looked extremely focused.

About twenty minutes before kickoff, my cell phone chirped. Debra and the girls were waiting at the pass gate for their tickets, which I had picked up at will-call. Dick went off to find his seat, and I went to get everyone into the stadium.

Upon our return, our section was filling with Pittsburgh fans, many dressed in the black-and-gold jerseys of their favorite players. They also clutched their Terrible Towels.

As we squeezed into our seats, a jeering voice rose in the air.

"Hey, you from Texas?"

I wondered how he knew—but then I remembered I was wearing a soiled white hat with a burnt orange Longhorn on the front. Only one of the most recognizable mascots in the nation.

"Yeah," I said, tugging on the bill of my cap.

Another guy—who had probably tailgated a bit too much already—entered the fray. "Nothing but steers and queers in Texas!" he yelled.

I looked at Debra, who rolled her eyes. It was going to be a long afternoon. This fellow obviously wasn't a Longhorn lover or a Cleveland fan.

"Whaddya doin' here?" asked another fan.

"My son is playing for Cleveland—"

"You must be Colt McCoy's dad."

The Pittsburgh fan had put two and two together rather quickly. "That would be me," I said.

The fan turned to his buddies in our section. "Hey, did you hear that? Colt McCoy's father is sitting with us today."

"And his mom and his wife," I said. Debra was seated to my left and next to Rachel.

Well, volunteering that information was like throwing meat to hungry lions. As word spread through our section that the McCoy family was in the Steelers fans' midst, we heard more trash talk.

"Polamalu is going to kill your son. I wouldn't watch if I was you," yelled one yahoo.

"You better hope Colt's life insurance is paid up today," jeered another.

We heard meaner taunts, but there were also Pittsburgh fans in our vicinity who were respectful and complimentary of Colt. Some wished us good luck, and obviously, we appreciated that. As for the trash talk, we shrugged that off. A security guard dropped by at one point and asked us if we were having any trouble with the fans, but we told him we were fine. Compared with what went on at a Texas-Oklahoma game, this was child's play.

Besides, what were our options? These were our seats, and we happened to be surrounded by Steelers fans. As the cliché goes, we were in *their* house—although I made a mental note to leave my Texas ball cap at home for future road games.

Colt

I felt good warming up and was eager for the opening kickoff. The Steelers chose to have their starting offense introduced before the game, giving their fans a chance to loudly cheer the return of Ben Roethlisberger. He ran out on the field wearing a Steelers "throwback" uniform from the 1960s—yellow helmet with a black stripe, a black No. 7 jersey with his number, name, and stripes all in yellow, and white pants with a single yellow stripe running down the length.

We won the toss and elected to receive. One of the big differences between college football and the pros, at least for quarterbacks, is how we receive the play calls from our coaches. At Texas, I looked to the sidelines, where three different players contorted their arms in various positions to signal in the play; only one player was "hot"—meaning he alone was signaling in the play.

In the NFL, it's entirely different. Quarterbacks have headsets in their helmets so they can listen for the plays called in from the sidelines. We don't have a microphone in our helmets, so we can't answer, but we do hear the play the head coach or the offensive coordinator calls in.

With the Browns, Coach Daboll relayed the plays into my helmet. Starting from our 35-yard line, I heard the first play call— a rollout pass. Instead of a tame handoff for my baptismal play from scrimmage, Coach wanted me to go at them. He wasn't sending me into the ring and telling me to clinch and cover up. Coach wanted to come out swinging and get an early completion. He had told me on the bus drive to Pittsburgh that he wanted to get the ball out of my hands so that I could get into rhythm early in the game. We were going to throw it around, not sit back and hand off.

I assumed my position under center, took the snap, rolled out to my right, and spotted receiver Brian Robiskie in the flat. We played pitch and catch for an eight-yard gain. Two plays after we earned a first down, we faced a third-and-10 from our 45-yard line, a passing situation. Even though blitzing linebacker James Harrison steamrolled me in the pocket as I got off the pass, I found our backup tight end, Evan Moore, for 19 yards, taking us down to the Pittsburgh 36-yard line. Our offense ran back to the huddle with extra spring in its step.

The Steelers responded by ratcheting up the pressure. On the seventh play of the drive, Pro Bowl linebacker LaMarr Woodley sacked me. Even though that created a second-and-19 passing situation, we stayed in aggressive mode. I threw to my right into triple coverage, but the pass bounced off the shoulder pads of my tight end, Ben Watson, and sprung into the air. With so many defenders around, the ball was easy pickings for Pittsburgh safety Ryan Clark.

Brad

Usually, a rookie quarterback crumbles after a setback like that. I've seen it happen a hundred times. And the Pittsburgh fans in our section, who had been pretty quiet after Colt's 19-yard pass on third down, loved their change of fortune. They rubbed it in pretty good.

Colt

I know how an early interception can set the tone for the game. That thought flashed through my mind, but I knew I had to find a way to let it go. I focused on the positives. Before the interception, we had moved the ball down the field, so I knew we could do it again.

Then our No. 1 pick in the 2010 draft, cornerback Joe Haden, returned the favor and made *his* first NFL interception. Better yet, he ran the ball back 62 yards into Pittsburgh territory. When our drive stalled, Phil Dawson booted a field goal, and we took a 3–0 lead. The score stayed that way until the second quarter, when the Pittsburgh offense came to life and scored a touchdown. It was still a game at halftime; we went into the locker room trailing 7–3.

Brad

As a coach, I was looking at the Steelers' defensive schemes. The Browns were missing some key players due to injury, and I wondered if the guys taking their places would hold their own.

Meanwhile, I watched Colt run the offense. I wondered: *Is he doing things right? Is he making good reads? Is he throwing to the right part of the field?* The dad part of me overshadowed a lot of that though. Inside, I rooted for my son to be successful, to complete passes, to not get hit, and to stay off the ground. I was emotionally hanging on every play.

I had good reason to be concerned because what unfolded was an unusually violent contest, even by NFL standards. James Harrison knocked wide receiver Joshua Cribbs out of the game after he replaced Colt at quarterback for one of those "wildcat" plays where a running back or receiver lines up in the shotgun formation to take the snap. After taking a snap, Joshua rolled to the right and then was nailed with a helmet-to-helmet hit from Harrison.

Later Harrison sent shock waves throughout the stadium—and the NFL, I later learned—when he flattened Browns wide receiver Mohamed Massaquoi with another devastating, helmet-to-helmet hit. Mohamed was really laid out on that play and suffered a concussion from the bone-crunching collision. There were no flags on either play, which infuriated the Cleveland bench. (Several days later, Harrison's on-the-field violence prompted Commissioner Goodell to impose a $75,000 fine as part of a league-wide crackdown on high hits to the head and neck.)

Even though Colt had lost his two top receivers, he continued to handle the pressure well, even after taking some good shots himself. Meanwhile, the fans around us egged on Harrison and company. Normally, fans yell, "Sack the quarterback!" but in Pittsburgh, it was "*Kill* the quarterback!" They wanted knockout shots.

To Debra and me, though, they were talking about knockout shots on *our son*. As a coach, I'd been around those types of fans, but as a mom, Debra hadn't sat with a boisterous crowd like that. At one point, she whispered to me that she had never seen such blood-thirsty people in her life.

Rachel was quiet, too, and kept her emotions in check. She and Deb comforted each other, and all three of us were encouraged to see Colt play pretty well, especially because the Browns often started with poor field position. It seemed like Colt began each offensive series around the Browns' 15- or 20-yard line, and then he would take the offense inside Pittsburgh territory to the 45- or 40-yard line, where the drive would stall and the Browns would be forced to punt. The game didn't get away from Cleveland until the fourth quarter, when Big Ben found his rhythm and led the Steelers to a big 21–3 lead.

Colt then engineered a six-play, 70-yard drive that was a thing of beauty. He hit receivers for 23 yards and 28 yards before tossing his first NFL touchdown. Even the Pittsburgh fans in our section gave us high fives and congratulatory wishes.

"No rookie has ever come in here and done this!" said one Pittsburgh supporter.

"Your son is unbelievable!" exclaimed another.

They could afford to be cordial because there were only four minutes left on the clock and the Steelers led comfortably. Obviously, if Colt's team had been in a position to win the game, they wouldn't have been so complimentary.

Colt

After time ran out in our 28–10 defeat, I walked onto the field to congratulate the winners. The protocol is for the starting quarterbacks to look for each other and exchange a handshake and a word or two. Big Ben found me first. With a white towel draped around his neck and a turned-around ball cap atop his head, he drew me close. "Great job," he said. "I thought you played well today. Keep your head up. You're going to be a great player."

I appreciated his words and jogged off the field. Soon it was time to face the media in the locker room. A reporter asked me what I thought of my play that day, and I replied that we didn't like the final result but that no one guy is going to win or lose a game for us. The credit had to go to the Pittsburgh defense because every time we got into the Steelers' half of the field, they stiffened.

"Do you feel ready to be a full-time quarterback in the NFL?" asked one reporter.

"I'm ready to do what this teams needs," I replied. "We'll move on week to week and evaluate Jake and Seneca. But, yeah, I feel really good."

Brad

We waited nearly an hour outside the fence between the fans and the team buses. One by one, the Browns players came out, and Colt was one of the last to emerge from the locker room.

Since we didn't have passes, Colt came outside the fence and hugged Rachel, then his mom.

"What did you think about the game?" he asked me.

"I thought you did great." Although the Browns lost decisively, the team had handled itself well in a tough environment, and Colt had led the offense up and down the field pretty well. (I learned after the game that he'd completed 23 of his 33 passes for 281 yards and one touchdown.)

"Yeah, but I wish I could have those two turnovers back."

"You were going for it. They were tipped balls. Happens to the best of them."

"I could have done some things better. I'm going to be better next week."

"And you will."

More hugs—and photo ops—were exchanged, and then Colt had to get on the team bus. We waved good-bye as the buses pulled away and headed toward Cleveland.

On the flight back to Texas, I looked out the window and let my thoughts wander. *Wow! That really happened—my son played an NFL game against the Pittsburgh Steelers.*

That had been Colt's lifelong goal. When he was in junior high and high school, he had told me he wanted to play quarterback at a Division I school and then play in the NFL.

Dad, I'm going to do this. I'm going to win a national champion-ship in college. I'm going to play in the NFL someday. This is what I want to do.

And he worked incredibly hard to make it happen.

In the days that followed, I went online and read some of the "reviews"—as well as what some of Colt's teammates had said about his first start.

James Walker of ESPN.go.com, wrote: "I've seen a lot of quar-terback debuts up close as a former Cleveland Browns beat writer, and Colt McCoy's first NFL start was the best of the group. McCoy, Cleveland's 16th starting quarterback since 1999, threw for 281 yards and one touchdown . . . . McCoy took a pounding and made rookie mistakes, but he also showed toughness, leader-ship and good accuracy."

That was nice to read, but what stood out even more to me were some of the things Colt's teammates said after the game.

"He's taken on the leadership role and is not afraid to direct the huddle, get control of it," said Browns' guard Eric Steinbach. "That's what a quarterback has to do."

"It was hard to even tell this was his first game," tight end Evan Moore said after the game. "He has a way about him. He has a presence. He's a natural-born leader."

And then I read about the "hay's in the barn" speech Colt delivered before the team on Saturday night—how he wasn't scared to play against the Steelers and that he couldn't wait to get out on the field with his teammates.

I shook my head in admiration. There was nothing cocky about what he said; he was just letting his teammates know they didn't have to worry about him and that he would be ready to play. In other words, he showed incredible leadership when most rookies would have been scared spitless.

Where did he get the idea to say those things? He certainly hadn't talked to me before the team bus left for Pittsburgh.

And then I smiled.

You see, I knew Debra and I had been preparing him for that moment since the day he was born.

For us, the hay was in the barn.

CHAPTER 2

A Tall Texas Tale

Colt

If you want to understand how I was raised, you need to understand how my father was raised—and his father before him.

You see, my grandfather, Burl McCoy, has been a great influence on my life. He's the patriarch of the family and a man I love, admire, and respect. You would, too, if you got to know him.

When most people hear the last name "McCoy," they think of the famous Hatfield-McCoy feud and wonder if I'm related to *those* McCoys. I don't think so. Both clans lived along the Kentucky–West Virginia border, where they clashed and feuded in the 1870s, but our branch of the McCoy family, as far as we can figure, did not come from the Appalachian backcountry.

Daddy Burl, as I call my grandfather, says his father—named Hollis McCoy—was born in 1903 outside of Abilene, Texas. When Hollis was three years old, his father rode off into the sunset, which is another way of saying that Jobe McCoy abandoned his family. "He was a scoundrel," my grandfather says.

Hollis had an older sister, an older brother, and a younger sister. If a couple of uncles had not come to their rescue, the abandoned family would likely have starved to death back in 1906 because there was no "safety net"—no welfare, food stamps, or housing subsidy programs to help people in such situations.

As you can imagine, Hollis had a rough childhood. By the time he was fourteen, he was on his own, farming and running land, doing what he could to survive. He became a sharecropper, which meant he rented land that he either cultivated or ranched on. Just after World War I, Hollis began working the north side of Taylor County, outside of Abilene.

Although he was a good farmer, Hollis gravitated toward the cattle business. Back then there were no livestock auctions between Fort Worth, Texas, and Clovis, New Mexico, so he'd go from ranch to ranch and buy three or four cows and figure out a way to get them to the slaughterhouses in Fort Worth. He became pretty good at guessing the weight of each steer and what each head would bring at auction. Hollis became quite a stockman.

But nothing was easy. Remember, Hollis was ranching and farming during the Great Depression and Dust Bowl days, when severe dust storms devastated prairie lands in Oklahoma and the Texas panhandle. In those dark times, Hollis brought home a dollar a day, two dollars if he purchased livestock at the right price.

Hollis McCoy understood the value of a buck. During the Depression, if something could be repaired, reused, rehemmed, or resewn, then that's what you did. His motto was "Make do and don't throw anything away." He lived frugally all his life. In fact, he didn't even want to spend the money on a telephone, calling it an intrusive "modern contraption" and a "waste of money." Hollis finally relented in 1955 and installed his first phone in his home. Hollis was fifty-two years old by then, and for the rest of his life, he never got used to talking on a telephone.

Hollis raised two sons. His youngest, my grandfather Daddy Burl, was born in 1933, in the midst of the Depression. My grandfather got started early working on the farm. By the time he was seven years old, he would mount a horse and help his father drive steers from Mr. Smith's place or Mr. Jones' place to a central lot, where the steers would be penned up until a truck arrived to load them up for the drive to the Fort Worth stockyards.

Daddy Burl grew up near Merkel, twenty miles west of Abilene.

His parents weren't churchgoers but were "clean livers," which is what people who didn't smoke, drink, or chew tobacco were called in those days. On Sunday mornings, my grandfather hunted for rabbits instead of going to Sunday school.

One time, when my grandfather was in his early teens, his older brother Gerald left the house to play in a weekend-long baseball tournament in Merkel, which was about seven or eight miles away. On this particular occasion, he stayed in town and spent the night with one of his aunts, who invited Gerald to go to church on Sunday morning. Gerald, who had always been interested in spiritual matters, eagerly said yes.

Gerald heard the Gospel preached that day, and the more he learned about who Jesus Christ was and how He came to this earth to die for our sins so that we could have eternal life, the more he wanted to go to church. Gerald invited his brother—Daddy Burl—to join him at church.

And that's where my spiritual lineage begins.

When Gerald and Daddy Burl became Christians, their parents noticed the differences in their lives and in their attitudes. Though my grandfather's mother was a Christian when she married Hollis, she confessed she had been away from the Lord all those years and wanted to get back on the straight and narrow path.

Hollis wasn't so sure. Abandoned by his father and raised in a broken home, he was a strong-willed, self-made man who resisted "religion," as he called it. After a series of great talks with his sons, though, Hollis said, "Yeah, I gotta do it." That's when my great-grandfather was baptized and became a Christian.

Daddy Burl was a good athlete. He tried his hand at football at Merkel High, but injuries kept him from playing much. The sport he excelled at was basketball, and he became one of the best players for counties around. But he also loved to run track. When track season came around one spring, he wanted to try the hurdles, but his track coach—who was also the Merkel High basketball coach—told him, "I don't have time to help you become a hurdler. I'll take you to the meets, but I'm not going to coach you. If you want to run the hurdles, you'll have to figure it out yourself."

Despite the lack of instruction, Daddy Burl qualified for the state track meet in Austin. A week before he was scheduled to run, he sought out a man named Oliver Jackson, Abilene Christian University's track coach, who was a legend in track circles. Daddy Burl was hoping for a few pointers from Coach Jackson, who had tutored several Olympians and always seemed to field powerful track teams at ACU. He agreed to take a look at Daddy Burl, but after watching him run a practice heat, the famed coach said, "Let's not change anything right before state. Otherwise, I'll just mess you up."

That introduction, however, was instrumental in leading Daddy Burl to enroll at Abilene Christian and run track for Coach Jackson, who must have been a great coach because he took my grandfather, a novice hurdler, and turned him into one of the top collegiate hurdlers in the country. Daddy Burl also had the talent to play on the ACU basketball team, where he showed his mettle on the hardwood.

"That was a tough double, playing basketball and then running hurdles," Daddy Burl said, "but I managed to have some great experiences."

I'll say. My grandfather's track teams won the NAIA national championship three years in a row, from 1952 to 1954, and in his senior season, he was the national champion in the 440-yard intermediate hurdles.

Daddy Burl sought out greater competition. In 1954 he finished second at the National AAU championships in St. Louis, losing to

Josh Culbreath, who set an American record that day and would go on to win a bronze medal in the 400-meter hurdles at the 1956 Olympic Games in Melbourne, Australia.

My grandfather would have qualified for the Olympics in Melbourne, but the National AAU held that because he coached a high school track team in 1955 for a $25 monthly stipend, he was a "professional" athlete and thus ineligible to compete for the U.S. Olympic team. Daddy Burl appealed, expressing contrition for being unaware of the rule and declaring that he would gladly give back his stipend, but the AAU governing board did not budge.

Brad

My father never complained about the raw deal he received, but he always regretted not knowing the rules and never getting to see if he could have won an Olympic medal. Four years later, a long jumper in Tennessee ran afoul of the same rules, but the AAU let him go to the Olympics in Rome. That ended the cycle.

My father started courting his future wife, Jan Gibson, while they both attended Abilene Christian. She was so well liked that she was voted homecoming queen her senior year. They decided to tie the knot in 1958, and I was born a year later at a country doctor's clinic in Merkel, a sleepy town with a population of a thousand people scattered on ranches and farms around a small downtown. I was the oldest of three; I'm two years older than Amy and six years older than Michael.

We were a working-class family of farmers and ranchers. We were up at dawn and in bed early. To keep food on the table, Dad moved back and forth between two worlds: ranching or farming and coaching. Dad, who had gotten the coaching bug after his college basketball and track days were over, had to carve out time to coach high school basketball and track.

There was still plenty of work to get done on Daddy Hollis' various ranch and farming operations. Over the years, he bought up chunks of land when he could—bartering with cattle or trading his services. Let's face it: land was pretty cheap during the Depression years and remained that way well into the 1950s. By the time I came along, the McCoy family owned a 150-acre wheat farm outside of Merkel, a 200-acre cotton farm in a small community known as Hodges, and a wheat farm and ranch at a 344-acre property that we called the Home Place, also near Merkel. Then my father purchased a 150-acre wheat farm that adjoined the Home Place, but my parents eventually built a home on the main property. They still live there today.

My father taught me—and later my younger brother, Michael—from a young age how to farm. I can remember how one time, when I was ten years old, Dad took me out to the back forty and plowed the perimeter of the field while I rode on the back of the tractor. Once he was done outlining the field, he jumped off the tractor and said I could plow the rest. He left me with a sack lunch, and I carefully plowed row after row until he came back for me at dusk. I did that every summer, starting after school got out in May, the time when we had to keep the fields tilled and the weeds down before the next planting.

You may be wondering, *How could your father be so cruel, leaving you out in the hot sun, driving that tractor all day? Weren't there child labor laws?*

Not when you're the son. Besides, I grew up understanding that I was required to help out on the family ranch. When Daddy Hollis was around, I learned that he was a no-nonsense taskmaster. I didn't mind, though, because I always knew where I stood with him. It also certainly helped that I grew to love working the land. Farm life has a wonderful rhythm that's hard to explain to city folk.

If you've ever lived on a ranch or a farm, you know there's always work to do. Even during the school year, we had to do chores. We still had cattle that needed to be tended to. We raised chickens, so there were always eggs to gather. We even kept a cow that had to be milked every morning.

It's not like I was a slave, however. Once we finished our work, we'd go fishing or hunting—or on vacation. Every June, after the wheat harvest, my parents took the family on a two-week trip to California to visit my mom's side of the family. We'd go to Disneyland and the beach, and we always spent a few days in Yosemite National Park for a Church of Christ family encampment. Between three thousand and six thousand people—men, women, and children—would camp in Yosemite and listen to singers and great speakers during the day and at evening gatherings.

By this time, after his mentor, Oliver Jackson, had retired, my father had become the assistant track coach at Abilene Christian. The ACU athletic director thought Dad could do a little ambassador work while he was at Yosemite, flying the purple Wildcats flag and talking up ACU.

"How can I do that?" my father asked. "I'm just a coach."

Then Dad came up with an idea: form a singing group and perform in front of the thousands attending the Yosemite encampment. Dad had started singing in the church when he was a youngster, and he and Mom really enjoyed singing.

So Dad and Mom enlisted the three kids and we formed a group that sang a cappella, meaning we sang without musical accompaniment, which is in keeping with the tradition of the Church of Christ. Dad and Mom put together a singing program that included some great old-time hymns as well as a few songs Mom wrote.

We called ourselves the McCoy Family Singers. In a sense, we were a church version of the von Trapp family of *The Sound of Music* fame. We were unique, we sounded fairly good, and people liked us. After singing for the first time in front of thousands at Yosemite, we drove back to Texas, where we received dozens of letters from churches and family conferences asking us to sing at their events. Since then, the McCoy Family Singers have performed all across the country, mainly during summers and holidays. We made a return engagement to Yosemite every June—until the U.S. Forest Service didn't renew the permit for the Church of Christ encampment. (That's a whole other story.)

Church and church social activities were very important to our family. Dad and Mom taught us that the most important things in life were our relationship with God and being servants to others. We were in church on Sunday mornings, Sunday nights, and Wednesday nights. If there was a church meeting or a fellowship gathering, we were the first ones there and the last ones to leave. If tables or chairs needed to be set up or taken down, we did that. If a meal was involved, we helped with the setup and stood behind the serving trays to dish out the food. We were always the last ones in line to eat, but we never lingered because there was cleanup to do. We turned off the lights and locked the doors.

That's how my parents raised me—to serve others.

During my elementary school years, we moved to Abilene because Dad was teaching PE classes at ACU in the morning and coaching the track team in the afternoon. When track practice was over, Dad and I would drive out to one of the farms before the sun went down to feed the cows, change an irrigation pipe, and repair fences before driving back to Abilene for supper.

After a while, my father thought about all the traveling we did and said to himself, "This is crazy." So he built a home at the Home Place. The move back to Merkel put me into the local schools, and when I reached high school age, I attended Merkel High School, a small school in Texas. There were about fifty students in my class.

I loved playing sports, and football was my favorite. But just like my father, I also played basketball and ran track. I played receiver on our football team, and I had good hands and caught the ball well. Back then I had the same dream as Colt: play Division I football and go on to the NFL. But in my senior year of high school, I suffered a horrible knee injury in the second game of the season. This was in 1977, before minimally invasive arthroscopic surgery became commonplace, so my dream of playing Division I football was done. Some big schools had been recruiting me, but once I tore up my medial collateral ligament (MCL), all the schools stopped recruiting me.

Except for one. The folks at ACU still liked me—they obviously knew the McCoy family—so they offered me a partial scholarship to play football. That worked for me. I didn't play much my freshman year because I was still rehabbing my knee, but I worked hard and, for the last half of my college career, I played some good ball.

Right about this time, Title IX began having a big impact in college athletics. Title IX, passed by the U.S. Congress in 1972, mandated that no person attending a school that received federal aid could be discriminated against on the basis of gender. Although there was no mention of sports in the landmark legislation, college athletic departments around the country began "leveling the playing field" and offered more women's sports.

The people at ACU looked around and decided they needed a women's basketball team pronto, so they asked my father to become the school's first women's basketball coach. In 1976 he gladly accepted the offer. Four years later, a young woman named Debra Woodruff contacted my father about playing ball for him. She had been an all-state basketball player at her high school in Atlanta, but her parents wanted her to attend Harding University, a Christian college in Arkansas. Harding didn't have a women's basketball team, but she followed her parents' wishes and enrolled there anyway. During her freshman year, Debra greatly missed playing basketball, so she asked her parents if she could transfer to a Christian college that had a women's basketball program.

"Come on down," my father said after hearing that Debra was a great defensive guard who could run the court. Debra accepted a partial scholarship offer and transferred to Abilene Christian.

One day, midway through Debra's first season at ACU, I happened to drop by Moody Coliseum to touch base with Dad. I first saw her, not from across a room, but from across a basketball court. I couldn't keep my eyes off her. I turned to a buddy who had accompanied me that day. "That's the one right there," I said, pointing to the cute girl with a ponytail and great legs. "I think I'll just marry that one."

I asked her out a couple of times, but she played hard to get with me. I told her she would get more playing time if she dated the coach's son, but even that line didn't work. Finally, she broke the ice by inviting me to be her Sadie Hawkins date. We really hit it off that evening. Spiritually, we were in sync, too.

We were sophomores at the time and quite infatuated with each other, but we had some minor breakups every summer when she'd go home to Atlanta and I'd head to the tractor seat on the farm. She had been raised in the same kind of hardworking family as I had . . . except for the farming part of it. Her father had come home from the Korean War and took a job selling shoes at a J. C. Penney store, and from there he worked his way up the corporate organizational chart until he took a top executive position with the well-known department store chain. He even befriended James Cash Penney himself.

When Debra and I returned to the Abilene Christian campus every fall, we would pick up where we left off. She could out-shoot me when we played H-O-R-S-E (you know, the basketball shooting contest where you get a letter for every shot you miss), and we both loved the outdoors. Debra had learned a love for fishing from her father, so going on a fishing trip to the family farm was always a fun date.

We talked often about marriage during college, but I never asked her. After we graduated, I stayed for a year at Abilene Christian to work as a graduate assistant on the football team—my entry into coaching—and Debra took a job coaching basketball at a public high school in Fort Worth.

We stayed in touch throughout the first half year after college, but I missed her greatly. Just before Christmas, I thought, *Have you lost your mind, letting this girl get away?*

I had come to my senses. I bought a ring, and after Christmas I traveled to Atlanta to ask Debra's father for his daughter's hand. After he gave me his blessing on New Year's Eve, I asked Debra to marry me. We got married on June 30, 1984. But like just about every happy-in-love young couple, we had no idea what the future held.

Colt

My parents waited a year and a half after they got married before Mom became pregnant with me in early 1986. By that time, they had moved to Lovington, New Mexico, where Dad had taken his first coaching position—at Lovington High, the only high school in the town of Lovington. The enrollment at Lovington High was around seven hundred students in a small city of twelve thousand. He was the football team's offensive coordinator and also taught

English classes as well as the journalism class, which put out the school newspaper once a month.

I'm sure Dad had to swallow some Longhorn pride to take a coaching job in New Mexico, but he was taking the long view. Dad saw Lovington as a solid first rung on the coaching ladder. I also suppose he had a good feeling about the high school because Lovington's mascot was the same as Abilene Christian's: the Wildcats.

Besides, Dad could always remind himself that the Lone Star State wasn't too far away. Located in the southeastern corner of New Mexico, Lovington—which billed itself as the Queen City of the Plains—was a twenty-mile straight shot to the Texas border on Highway 82.

But we still weren't in Texas. When Mom became pregnant, her doctor told her they would be delivering the baby at Lea Regional Medical Center in Hobbs, twenty miles to the southeast of Lovington, but still in New Mexico. Hobbs was fifteen miles from the Texas border.

According to a Texas-sized tall tale, Mom was in labor with me for more than twenty hours—sorry, Mom!—but Dad had planned all along for me to be born in Texas. When he couldn't talk Mom into going across the border somewhere in Texas, he had to think of something fast. He made a mad twenty-mile dash to the West Texas plains around Denver City and filled a shoe box with good ol' Texas dirt. As Mom was wheeled into the delivery room, Dad slipped the shoe box under the delivery table, and there you have it: I was born on Texas soil.

I first heard this crazy story around 2008, when an enterprising reporter unearthed the "Shoe Box of Texas Soil" story. For a couple of days after practice, I had microphones and TV cameras thrust in my face, asking me if this story was true.

I played along. "How could I know?" I said. "I was busy getting born. But that's what my dad says. Nobody says it wasn't true, so I guess it's true."

Brad

We kept it a secret from Debra for a long time. It's become one of those deals where I may have to go to my grave before anyone really knows if it's true or not. But Debra could hardly believe it when the story broke a few years ago. I guess you could say I hid things for many years. It's hard to tell your wife there was a shoe box filled with dirt underneath the bed where she had given birth to her first child.

Colt

I think I know why my dad went to all that trouble. It was important to him—and the family—that I be born in Texas. My dad had grown up in Texas, so he must have had this crazy thought: *I'm going to name my son Colt, and he's going to be a quarterback at Texas, and I can't let people know he was born in New Mexico.* I guess since Dad had this thought, I had to be a Texan.

Brad

Debra and I did not know we would be having a boy. We could have found out during her pregnancy because she had several ultrasound tests, but we asked the doctor not to tell us. We were old-school and didn't want to know. So it was a wonderful surprise when our firstborn child was a boy and came into this world—with a healthy set of lungs—on September 5, 1986.

It was my idea to name our son Colt, although Debra had to sign off on it. When I'm out speaking, people often ask where the name Colt came from, and what I say is that I didn't know anyone else named Colt but that I always thought it would be a cool name for my son. Colt had an outdoorsy, life-on-the-ranch feel to it, probably because the traditional definition of the word *colt* is a young male horse under the age of four. There was also a famous pistol known as the Colt .45, which had been popular in Texas since the nineteenth century.

But those aren't the only reasons I liked the name Colt. I was probably most influenced by the TV series *The Fall Guy*, which ran on ABC from 1981 to 1986, the year of Colt's birth. The show was about the adventures of a Hollywood stuntman named Colt Seavers, who moonlighted as a bounty hunter. The star was Lee Majors, the former Six-Million Dollar Man.

So Colt would be his name. But what about a middle name?

We also wanted to name our son Daniel after the Old Testament prophet. The book of Daniel tells the story of how the prophet was carried off from Israel to Babylon at a young age. But Daniel always remained true to God, despite living in a foreign land where the people worshipped pagan deities. When King Darius threw Daniel into the lions' den for continuing to worship his God, the lions didn't harm him, which was a testament to Daniel's faithfulness.

Debra and I didn't like the way "Colt Daniel McCoy" sounded, but we did like the way "Daniel Colt McCoy" came off the tongue, so we went with the latter construction on his birth certificate. So, technically speaking, Colt is Colt's middle name, though few people know that.

Colt

I didn't have anything to say about my name, of course, but I really like it. For sure, the name Colt is becoming more popular. In fact, those who track such things—like the Social Security Administration, which compiles a list of baby names—say that Colt was the 370th most popular baby name in 2009, a big jump from the 909th in 2006, when I was in my redshirt freshman season at the University of Texas.

Over the past couple of years, I've met a ton of parents who've named their sons Colt, and these meetings usually happen at random times: walking around Austin, or in hotels and restaurants throughout Texas. I can't tell you the number of times my wife, Rachel, and I have been out for dinner when a young father or mother drops by our table to say, "We named our son Colt. He's doing great. He's two years old."

When these parents have their Colt with them, they often ask me to pose for a picture with him or sign something. I've received stacks and stacks of fan mail with similar requests. All the children with the name Colt seem to be one, two, or three years old—infants, toddlers, and preschoolers.

But here's a different story. Rachel and I were eating in an Austin restaurant one evening when something caught my eye a few tables away. A small boy, probably a year old, was sitting in a high chair wearing a No. 12 University of Texas jersey.

That was my number at Texas.

"There's another kid named Colt," I said to Rachel, who glanced over her shoulder. The parents noticed us looking their way, and they giggled a bit. My wife and I both knew what was coming: a visit from these folks.

They waited until we were done with our meal, and they were very polite when they approached us. The mother cradled the bouncing infant who was wearing the white Texas jersey in her arms. "This is our son, and his name is McCoy."

"Really?" I was genuinely surprised. This was the first time I'd met parents who named their son after my *last* name.

"Yeah," said the father, "we heard of a lot of parents calling their baby boys Colt, but we want his name to be unique, so we named our baby McCoy. That's his first name."

That was unique, all right. I thought maybe McCoy was his middle name, but I was wrong. Maybe they'll call him Coy. I had heard of parents giving their children unusual names over the years, like the couples who've named their children Espn—after the cable sports network—and pronouncing it *Espen*. To me, naming a boy McCoy seemed to be, well, in the same ballpark.

I must confess that the idea that thousands of parents have named their sons Colt is rather mindboggling to me. I never expected this when I started playing football, even at Texas. At the same time, hearing about all the Colts out there motivates me to protect my name.

Here's what I'm thinking: *Since a lot of families have named their son Colt, I don't want to mess that up for them. I don't want to be a guy who gets in trouble. I don't want to be the guy who is in the media for something negative. I want to live up to my name. I want to protect my name—for myself and for those children named Colt.*

Coming back to the theme of this book, whatever you choose to name your children—Colt, McCoy, or Espn—I can only hope and pray that you're preparing them for the path, not the path for them.

As you'll see in coming chapters, my parents *did* prepare me for the path, and sometimes they even put a few rocks and boulders in my way.

CHAPTER 3

GETTING WITH
THE FAMILY PROGRAM

Colt

Like most people, I don't remember much about my first few years of life. I certainly don't remember the first time I "performed" before thousands of people.

My earliest public appearance, I'm told, took place at Yosemite National Park during the 1987 Church of Christ family encampment. I was nine months old, and the McCoy Family Singers were nearing the end of their singing program. Dad, being a proud pop, asked Mom if she would come onstage, and bring me along, for the last number. With oohs and aahs coming from the crowd, Mom joined the chorus while I fidgeted in her arms before the thousands in attendance.

I was the first McCoy grandchild, so I imagine Dad was delighted to show off the "next generation" of the McCoy Family Singers. When I got older—say, by the time I reached first grade—I started singing with Dad, my grandparents Daddy Burl and GranJan (that is what we called our grandmother), Aunt Amy, and Uncle Michael. That was always near the end of the show during the "sing-along" numbers.

Back then I wasn't really aware of what I was doing; I sang because I was asked to. Truth be known, I was more interested in doing things like running my toy tractors through the dirt, finding sticks so I could have "sword fights," and playing anything that involved a ball.

Brad

Colt was full of energy and into typical boy mischief, but he was never mean-spirited. When he hit his toddler years, Debra and I noticed that he seemed to be a determined youngster. One time we drove to Daddy Burl's place for a long Easter weekend. Colt was two and a half, and we were still living in Lovington, New Mexico. I wanted to teach Colt a few things about fishing, so on Saturday morning I took him out to one of the ponds on Dad's property and showed him how to cast a line into the water. He loved the casting part, and when the fish started biting, he was hooked.

The next morning, Easter Sunday, we were all getting ready to go to church. My mother, Jan, was in the kitchen when she said, "Come, everyone. You have to see this."

Standing on the backyard porch was Colt, dressed in his Sunday best. I'm talking about a white seersucker suit with red suspenders, a white shirt, a thin black tie, and shiny Sunday shoes. Gripping a fishing rod in his small hands, Colt practiced cast after cast into the backyard.

"Go fishin'!" he said to anyone listening. "Go fishin'!"

In Colt's mind, he was getting himself ready to throw a line into the water. That was just like Colt. Whenever we taught him something athletic—like throwing a ball, shooting a basket, hitting a pitch—he always wanted to practice so he could get better.

Debra quit her job as the Lovington High School girls' basketball and track coach to be a stay-at-home mom with Colt, and I think that decision had a lot to do with how well he and his two younger brothers turned out. Living on one income—a high school coach and teacher's salary at that—wasn't easy, but it was well worth the investment. Our mind-set was that if we were going to have kids, then we wanted Mom home to raise them. Those were some tough years though.

Our family grew when our second son, William Chance McCoy, named after Debra's father, was born two years after Colt. I wanted to call him Willy, but Debra wouldn't go for that, so we settled on Chance. Our last child, Casey Burl McCoy, was born in 1991, making him five years younger than Colt. We named him after my father, and we called him Case.

Case arrived a couple of years after we moved the family back to San Saba, which is located right in the heart of Texas. I had accepted the head football coaching position at San Saba High School, a nine-through-twelve high school with an enrollment of around 250 students. Returning to Texas was the grand plan all along. It wasn't like I "heard Mama calling," as legendary Alabama football coach Bear Bryant said when he returned to his alma mater in 1957, but Texas was home.

San Saba High, with its small student body, was a Class 2A school. In Texas, high schools are placed in divisions according to enrollment. Class 1A schools are the smallest, with enrollments of less than 140 students, and Class 5A schools are the largest, with enrollments of more than 2,500—and some of the larger schools have twice as many students. The 5A schools were generally located in Texas' major cities, such as Dallas, Houston, San Antonio, Austin, and Odessa. This is where "Friday Night Lights" football is played before boisterous crowds of up to fifteen thousand spectators. Some high school stadiums even have high-tech scoreboards. When the demand for a local game is too high, the teams play at the nearest college stadium.

I didn't need the bright lights of the big city, though. Debra and I were more interested in quality-of-life issues and in raising our boys in a small-town environment. Moving to San Saba turned out to be a great move since it also brought us closer to the family homestead in Merkel. San Saba is only 110 miles from the Home

Place, and we spent many three-day weekends and school holidays with Daddy Burl and GranJan. When we visited my folks, I would run a tractor and help out Dad while the boys "explored" the ranch.

Being a high school teacher and coach, I was off during the summer months, but I couldn't afford not to work during that time. I got a job managing San Saba's municipal pool and organizing swimming lessons while Debra ran the concession shop. The boys were in the water all day long, but before they grew gills, we found a place in my office where they could nap.

The municipal pool closed at 6:00 p.m., but my day didn't end there. Many nights after dinner, I would meet some of my high school players at a nearby ranch and we'd haul hay into barns for several hours. Colt joined me on occasion, too, and he helped where he could. I let him drive the truck slowly while we threw the hay onto the trailer. He was just six or seven years old at the time.

Working two jobs during the hot summer months—and Texas is *sweltering* in June, July, and August—was what I had to do to make ends meet. But even though money was tight in those days, I wouldn't have changed a thing. As far as I was concerned, there was no other job in the world where my kids could be such a close part of my life. That's why I made a conscious decision to coach and teach at smaller schools. I had received some feelers from colleges and the large metropolitan 5A schools, but I preferred living in small-town Texas, where life was slower and the outside influences on the boys were easier to deflect or manage.

It helped that I was used to living in hamlets with one elementary school and one junior high and one high school—one-stoplight towns where everybody knew everybody. Small-town life was comfortable to us, and being close to places where we could hunt for white-tailed deer and fish for bass was a bonus. Let's face it: I was a country boy, and I wanted Colt and his brothers to follow in their father's footsteps. We didn't even mind that everybody knew everybody's business, or that everybody in the local coffee shops and barber shops had an opinion about the local football coach.

Here's an example. When I started coaching the San Saba Fighting Golden Armadillos, I learned that Rogan Field was built over what used to be a cemetery, before it was converted into the high school football field in 1935. But not all the graves were removed, which meant there were still some Civil War skeletons resting underneath the sod.

Shortly after I arrived in San Saba, workers constructing a field house dug up pieces of old tombstones. More pieces of markers were unearthed when a new watering system was installed. When I asked why workers were finding bits of old tombstones, I was told that our football field used to be a cemetery and that back in the day, locals called our field "The Graveyard."

That gave me an idea. I had the Ag shop build a big wooden sign with the words WELCOME TO THE GRAVEYARD burned into the wood. My plan was to hang the sign over the entrance of Rogan Field. The women from the First Methodist Church across the street weren't amused when they saw the sign, but many of their husbands and sons had played there, and they thought it was a pretty cool ploy. We were even featured in *Sports Illustrated* that year because of the uniqueness of our football field.

Some interesting things happened during our home games. We started getting some freaky breaks. A player from the opposing team would catch a ball in the open field, have nothing but green grass ahead of him, and then suddenly trip and fall. Loose fumbles miraculously bounced our way. Holders mishandled routine snaps, causing their kickers to miss game-tying PATs, giving us the win.

These were normal things that happen in high school football games, but weird stuff happened so often that our opponents wondered if ghostly arms and hands were reaching up from their graves to help the hometown eleven. The Graveyard even gave new meaning to the football term *coffin corner* because it seemed like our punts always took a favorable bounce out of bounds inside the 10-yard line.

A 2A powerhouse and bitter rival, Goldthwaite High, who actually won a couple of state championships during this period, lost two straight times at the Graveyard following some crazy mishaps late in the games that sealed victories for the Armadillos. Goldthwaite coach Gary Proffitt and I were good friends, and he could never quite figure out if the Graveyard thing was the problem or if it just got into his kids' heads.

Which is why I had that sign put up . . . .

With the local ladies in an uproar, though, we had to move the WELCOME TO THE GRAVEYARD sign from the entrance to our field over to the visitor's locker room, where it wasn't visible to Sunday morning parishioners. The sign mysteriously disappeared the week after our annual grudge match with Goldthwaite—which we won 13–7—never to be seen again.

Colt

I was three years old when we moved from Lovington to San Saba, so I don't remember all the Graveyard stuff. Probably my earliest memories date back to kindergarten. I took the bus to school, and I can remember Mom and Chance greeting me at the bus stop when I came home. Case was an infant, so he would have been in a stroller or in my mother's arms. Chance was always excited to see me, and I was happy to see him (as well as Case) because we loved playing together.

When I started elementary school, there were days when I didn't ride the bus home but took a different bus that would drop me off at San Saba High School, where I'd run out to the football field. Dad would acknowledge my arrival and then blow his whistle to resume practice. I'd sit on the bench and do my homework, and then I'd watch Dad's teams scrimmage and run drills. Those were fun times, standing in the shadows of the varsity football players. They were so big and tall and hairy that they looked like gladiators to my first-grade eyes.

At first, all the players lining up and then crashing into each other confused me, but I soon figured out what was going on. My eyes were drawn to the quarterback, who seemed to be the center of attention. After calling for a huddle, the quarterback would yell funny-sounding numbers and words, and then with a "Hut-hut!" all sorts of chaos ensued.

In my world, quarterbacks were *the* guys, the big shots, the big men on campus. Right from the beginning, I saw how they made things happen on the field. Someday, I vowed, I would be one of them.

Inevitably during practice, some of the kids in the neighborhood who were close to my age would drop by the football field looking for a pickup game. We'd find a patch of grass beyond the end zone and play tackle football, which was fine with me. I never really liked touch football. If we didn't have a football, we'd put some rocks in a water bottle and use that as our ball. Our games were simple; we usually played a variation of the game called "tackle the man with the football." Even when just three or four kids showed up, we found a way to play.

Dad let me be the water boy during Friday night games, which was quite an honor for a kindergartner. I took my water boy duties very seriously, and that meant being close to the action. One Friday night, I was standing next to Dad when a sweep came our way. The fullback flattened me as he was driven out of bounds—and I ended up in the most pain I had ever felt, at least up to that point. I screamed and cried.

A hush came over the crowd. Mom came rushing out of the stands, and she and Dad asked me if I was all right. I tried to be as brave as I could, knowing that the players and everyone in the stands were watching. Mom rushed me to the emergency room while the game went on. The X-ray was easy to read—I had broken my collarbone. That night I learned an important lesson: collisions between little kids and big football players in helmets and pads weren't good. I thought I was old enough to take a hit, but I guess I wasn't.

As soon as I felt better, I returned to the sidelines. I wasn't afraid, but I kept a closer eye on running plays coming my direction. I loved being around the bench and all the excitement of a football game. I also loved the smells of the locker room—a combination of cut grass, sweaty uniforms, caked dirt, and tons of Icy Hot.

When games or practices weren't going on, I'd hang out in the coaches' office, where Dad and his assistants would draw up plays on the blackboard and debate whether the quarterback should throw the ball shallow to this player or throw the ball deep to that player.

This was my first exposure to the Xs and Os of the football world—Os being the offensive players and Xs representing the defensive players. Dad and his assistants used the letters to diagram plays on the chalkboard, and sitting off to the side of the room, I learned a lot of football by osmosis. I was really watching and seeing things. Of course, I could not call plays, but I was seeing how some plays developed. Watching college football games on TV every Saturday enhanced my football education. It seemed like the University of Texas was always playing on TV, and Dad often sat with me and explained what was going on.

By the time I was seven years old, I understood a lot more about what was happening on the football field. That's because I was at practice almost every day. I'd watch the offense run the same play over and over to get it right in practice, and I noticed that some plays seemed to work better than others.

When I hit elementary school, I graduated to ball boy. I took great pride in being the best ball boy in Texas. If it was raining, I made sure I kept those footballs dry. One night we were in the middle of a big game, struggling to get on track. Nothing we tried on offense seemed to be working. It was like we were snake bit.

Then I remembered a play that always worked in practice. I tugged at Dad's coat, but his eyes remained glued to the field. He was busy yelling instructions and encouragement to the offense.

"Daddy," I said, tugging at his coat one more time. "Daddy, run the screen. They can't stop it."

My father pulled his attention away from the field.

"What did you say, son?"

"Run the screen. They can't stop it."

Dad spoke into his microphone to his offensive coordinator, who was sitting in the ramshackle press box. "Colt wants to run the screen. What do you think?"

Dad listened on his headset. Then I heard him say, "Good deal. I'll signal it in."

Dad, who preferred to call his own plays, signaled "screen pass" to his quarterback. It was a third-and-long situation. The quarterback dropped back, dropped back farther, and then let the rush swarm him. Then, just before he was sacked, he flicked the ball to our halfback, who had nothing but daylight ahead of him. He didn't score on the play, but he ran for a huge first down that led to a touchdown and San Saba's first lead of the game—a game the Armadillos would go on to win.

Brad

I was in the heat of this high school battle, and then I'm looking at my six-year-old, who's telling me I should call a screen pass. Even then, he was a student of the game. He watched how things happened on the football field and seemed to have some smarts for the game.

I remember sitting in church one time when Colt was in the first or second grade. During the sermon, he showed me one of the coloring books the ushers had handed him to keep the kids occupied during the service. Colt had drawn up some plays. He had drawn Os and Xs in his coloring book. Sure, there may have been thirteen offensive players in on the play, but I could see he was starting to grasp the concept of the quarterback doing this and the wide receiver going there.

By the time Colt was eight or nine years old, he would sit in with me and my assistants in after-practice meetings, when we'd watch film and diagram new plays. He loved to show me the latest "trick" play he'd come up with. It was usually something along the lines of a motion reverse to the running back, who handed off to the wide receiver, who then threw back across the field to the quarterback, who was running down the field. The play resulted in the quarterback scoring a touchdown every time, and that quarterback would be Colt, naturally.

Now, you may be reading this and be thinking, *Is that all they talked about in the McCoy house—football?*

From August to early December, the answer would be yes. Okay, I'm joking. But I'm not joking when I say Debra and I took our roles as parents very seriously. We believed that God designed the family and that children thrived best in an atmosphere of genuine love, undergirded by reasonable, consistent discipline. We saw our duties as parents as imparting our spiritual values to the boys, providing strong leadership in the home, showing affection to each other as well as to the children, and teaching our children the value of hard work. And that was just the short list.

Colt was not a strong-willed child in the sense that he would clench his little fists and dare Debra or me to meet his challenges. But he showed great tenacity as a youngster, and every now and then, he wanted to find out what our boundaries were and what we'd do to enforce them.

Debra and I believed in spanking. Both of us had grown up with parents who meted out corporal punishment when the occasion warranted. "Spare the rod and spoil the child" was their guiding philosophy, and that became ours as Colt and the boys came along.

Now, did we *look* for reasons to spank Colt, just to make sure he learned discipline by the seat of the pants? Of course not. But we knew better than to depend on hope and luck to teach him and his brothers the critical attitudes we wanted to instill in our children. We carefully considered the times when a spanking was appropriate because we believed that, when properly applied, loving discipline works.

Debra and I always believed that on those occasions when we spanked Colt, we were drawn even closer to him—and he to us—because we comforted him in his tears. When the spanking was over, we reminded him that we loved him and that we wanted him to grow up to become the best he could be.

We saw the benefits of loving discipline in Colt's attitude. He never defied us. Disobeyed us on occasion? Sure. Make some poor decisions? Of course. But all in all, he grew up with the right attitudes. He learned fast.

Colt didn't get a lot of whuppings. The times we had to discipline him were few and became rarer as he grew older. Colt figured out our high expectations for him, and consequently, he had high expectations for himself.

Looking back, Debra and I are glad we administered loving discipline *early* in Colt's life because relatively speaking, we sailed through his teen years. Colt's teen years weren't as hard for us as they were for a lot of other parents we knew. Not to say that Colt didn't get into trouble or that he was a perfect kid, because he wasn't. But we certainly had an easier time than we otherwise would have.

You see, I saw the results of a lack of parental discipline every day on the practice field. I could tell which kids were never told no in their lives. They were used to doing exactly what they wanted to do.

Many of these kids came from homes where there were no curfews. Well, I had a curfew for my players: 10:00 p.m. on school nights and midnight on weekends. I caught some grief for that, especially at San Saba. Some of the parents said it wasn't my business. True, it wasn't my *personal* business, but it was my *professional* business, and that's how I decided to run our teams.

In 1994 the San Saba school board called me into one of its meetings. I had finished my fifth season of coaching the 'Dillos, and we'd had a strong season that took us into the state playoffs. I had a two-year contract with one year left. Normally, school boards automatically renew a coach's contract each year so that he always has a two-year contract. That way, if he has a bad season and the board wants to fire him, he has at least a one-year severance.

When I arrived at the board meeting, I was quickly informed

that San Saba wasn't going to renew my contract. I could remain as the football coach for one more year, but basically it was like a vote of no confidence. It's almost like they'd hung up a sign that said, "We'd like to fire you."

My first question was why the board wanted me gone, especially after we'd had such a great season.

"You're too tough on the kids," said the board president. "They're not having any fun."

I knew why they were saying I was too tough on the kids. That season, we had several code of conduct violations. Players broke team rules and school rules, so they were disciplined.

"Do you think we won all those football games because we were so talented?" I asked the board.

"Sure," one board member replied. "Any coach could win with the talent you had."

I knew better than that and tried to reason with them, as did some of my supporters in the community, but it was obvious they were not going to have any change of heart. I couldn't change the way I thought I should coach or my philosophy of growing young athletes. We were at an impasse, which wasn't good for anyone.

I requested that the board's decision be tabled with the promise that I would resign and take another job within six weeks.

I was gone in three.

Back in San Saba these days, they say that the Graveyard has lost its aura, that there's no home-field advantage like we had in the good old days. In those days, the Armadillos went to the playoffs, but for the past seventeen years, basketball season has started on schedule more often than not. I hear there's another new coach in town, and I hope he can bring the 'Dillos back to their old prominence. I cheer his efforts and wish him the best.

The San Saba story is one reason I always felt discipline was important for my football teams *and* for Colt and his brothers. Debra and I had a goal of raising our boys into young men who would love the Lord, be productive, and make great husbands and fathers one day.

You could say that we parented with purpose.

Colt

On this spanking thing, Mom and Dad may say I didn't get spanked that much, and they're probably right. But when you're a kid, it sure doesn't seem that way. I can remember both parents popping me on the bottom with a bare hand, Mom spanking me with a wooden spoon, or Dad spanking me with a belt. If we were outside, Dad sometimes used a switch.

Here's how I remember things: if I mouthed off to Mom or showed disrespect, she'd warn me to watch it. After the second warning—not the third or fourth—she'd march into the kitchen and grab the wooden spoon. And I'd get a couple of good whacks on the behind.

I soon learned that if I ever upset Mom to the point that she'd spank me, more wrath was waiting for me when Dad got home. Yes, I heard Mom say those dreaded words: "Wait until your father gets home." When I heard her say that, I knew I was in big trouble, and those afternoons never passed more slowly.

Dad would come home from practice, and after hearing Mom lay out the charges against me, he'd ask me if they were true. I knew resistance was futile. After I confessed my misdeeds, Dad would take me into my bedroom and spank me with the belt.

I later found out that Dad doesn't like to be reminded about these episodes. On one occasion, just after I started attending the University of Texas, he and I were asked to speak at a father-and-son gathering in Austin.

Dad and I stood next to each other, taking turns talking about our experiences together and the lessons we had learned while I was growing up. One of the things Dad discussed with the fathers in the room was the value of discipline and what it really means.

"Discipline is teaching. It's correcting. It's respect. It's all those things," he said. "Discipline is not going out there and beating your son whenever he does something wrong. Sure, I disciplined Colt, but I didn't *just* put the belt to him."

I raised my hand. "Hold on, Dad. I want to show everyone a verse in the Bible that you followed."

Dad had a quizzical look on his face, but I plowed ahead.

"If you brought your Bible with you, turn to Proverbs 23:13."

I waited for the men to find that passage of scripture, and then I read it aloud: "Do not withhold discipline from a child; if you punish them with the rod, they will not die."

Everyone in the crowd started laughing because they had caught on that my father wasn't the type to withhold discipline from me, and that meant he *did* discipline me with a belt. At the same time, everyone in the audience could see that I had not died.

I laughed right along with them.

But there was an occasion when I was spanked *outside* the home, and it wasn't any laughing matter. It happened when I was in the fourth grade at Hamlin Elementary School, where everyone knew each other.

I had a lot of friends, but there was one kid who really got on my nerves—and everyone else's. I'll call him Matt. He was not a bad person—just one of those kids who was a pest on the playground. Well, it was basketball season, and I was playing in an organized basketball league called Little Dribblers. In my class, the issue of who was on your team and who wasn't was very competitive. One of my best friends, Jimmy, was on my team, and he had a new pair of shoes, the fancy kind. This being the mid 1990s, they were Nike Air Jordans.

I did not have nice basketball shoes. I just played in whatever sneakers I had. Jimmy wore Air Jordans, which were far too expensive for Mom and Dad. That was okay because wearing the latest basketball sneakers wasn't important to me back in fourth grade.

Jimmy kept his Air Jordans in his school locker, and one day after class, he said he wanted to show them to me but not to Matt, the kid who got on everyone's nerves.

After Jimmy opened his locker, Matt saw him showing me his new shoes. Matt got jealous because he was excluded, and he really wanted to see the shoes—so he came over to Matt's locker. But Jimmy still held off—I suppose because he was trying to be mean to Matt.

Here's where I opened my mouth. "You can see the shoes tonight when we play and beat you all," I told Matt, who played on a different team.

My fourth-grade trash talk set him off. There was a push and a shove—nothing beyond the usual roughhousing I did at home with my younger brothers—but then Matt fell and screamed out in pain. He had broken his finger. I don't recall who pushed him to the floor, but I do remember that there were lots of tears. A couple of teachers broke up the scuffle and demanded an explanation of what had happened.

Matt and I were sent to the principal's office, but I wondered why *I* had to go. It was Jimmy who had said Matt couldn't see his new basketball shoes. I hadn't started anything.

At least, that's how I saw things. But I knew getting sent to the principal's office was serious stuff, even if I was innocent. I knew I would be in big trouble once Dad and Mom found out I was sent to the principal's office, guilty or not. *Colt, you're going to get the hugest spanking, and then you're going to be grounded for life,* I thought.

Once we were at the principal's office, we had what seemed like the longest wait ever—over an hour. Finally, the school secretary told us the principal wanted to see us but that he wanted to speak to Matt first. I watched Matt walk in. A few minutes later, he walked out with a relaxed smile on his face. He didn't say anything, but he had a look that said, *No big deal. You're going to be fine.*

I wasn't so sure. When it was my turn to see the principal, I felt more nervous than I had in my entire life.

"Okay, Colt, let's hear your side of the story," the principal began.

"Look, I really didn't do anything. I don't know how Matt broke his finger. I was just there."

The principal seemed to accept my explanation. In fact, he didn't say anything more or ask me any other questions. "Thank you for coming, Colt," he said. "You're dismissed."

I couldn't believe my good luck. Since nothing happened to me in the principal's office, I wouldn't have to take a note home to Mom and Dad. Maybe I wouldn't be grounded for life after all.

Dad was supposed to pick me up from school, so I walked out to the sidewalk to wait for him. Dad certainly seemed to be taking his time getting to school that day. Finally, just when I had lost hope that he was coming for me, he arrived in his pickup truck.

The passenger door popped open. "Get in the truck," said my father. He usually didn't give gruff commands like that. I hopped in, trying to put on a happy face and pretend nothing unusual had happened at school that day. *Surely he doesn't know anything,* I thought.

We drove home in silence. I tried to keep my composure because I felt there was no way my father could know I was in the principal's office just an hour before.

When we got home, Chance and Case were playing basketball in the backyard. I was just about to go outside when I heard Dad say, "Your mother and I would like to talk to you."

"About what?" I asked.

"About what happened at school today," my father said.

I looked to Mom, but she had the same stony look on her face as Dad.

"Have a seat, Son."

Dad and Mom drew the story out of me, and I told it the way I have described it in this chapter. They listened, and then Dad cleared his throat.

"Son, we treat everybody the right way around here. It doesn't matter if you like Matt or not. You will treat him the right way, and you will show everyone respect. That starts with your teachers but also includes your friends and people who are not even your friends. You will show everyone respect."

Mom added her two cents, and then my father solemnly announced that I would be punished for what happened. A spanking with the belt.

Dad whupped me pretty good that day, and I cried.

I went to school the next day thinking it was all over, but as soon as I stepped into the classroom, my teacher told me the principal wanted to see me in his office again.

My heart sank. *What did I do this time?*

I soon found out.

The principal was waiting for me in his office with a leather strap, and he explained that I needed to be punished for my role in hurting Matt. He gave me several licks, and I cried again. Then he told me that I would have to apologize to everybody in my class, telling them I was wrong to play favorites and that in the future I would respect everyone the same.

I remember the incident like it was yesterday. The lesson that I learned was this: if you don't like a kid, you don't tell him that to his face. You still have to treat him with respect. When you do that, you'll earn the same type of respect from everybody else.

By the way, it wasn't until years later that I learned Dad and the principal were buddies and they both agreed that I would get some licks at home *and* at school. But they taught me a lesson that I would never forget.

Brad

It may sound like we were too hard on Colt that day, or even like we were abusing him, but that's far from the truth. The fact is that Debra and I looked for those "teachable moments" that come up every now and then when you're raising children. God had given us the assignment of introducing our children to God's unfathomable love *and* justice. We knew that if we just loved our children but permitted them to treat us—or that boy who got on everyone's nerves—disrespectfully, then we would have failed to teach them the proper understanding of God's true nature.

So we had to draw a line in the dirt and instruct the children in what was and what wasn't acceptable behavior and attitudes. They learned that there were consequences when they crossed that line. Sometimes it was the belt, but other times they lost privileges. Whatever the infraction, we always tried to be consistent. That's because the line in the dirt always had to be in the same place.

Colt

I'll give my parents this: they *were* consistent. I always knew where I stood and what they expected of me. One of the things they were sticklers on was our language.

I was always taught to respect my elders and to say, "Yes, ma'am,"

"No ma'am" and "Yes, sir," "No, sir," when I addressed an adult. And don't even *think* of calling an adult by his or her first name.

This was mainly Mom's doing. She constantly reminded us that we had to careful about the words we chose to say.

There were words I was taught *not* to say, and the list was a lot longer than the usual four-letter words kids yell out in the school yard. I'm talking about words like *crap, fart*, and *shut up*. I couldn't even call one of my younger brothers "stupid" or "moron." I could call him a "dummy," but I couldn't call him stupid.

Since I couldn't tell Chance or Case to "shut up," I had to employ more polite expressions, such as "Will you please be quiet?" or "Please close your mouth."

By the time I got to school, I thought "shut up" and "stupid" were bad words. I didn't say them in the classroom, and I certainly didn't say them around Mom and Dad because if I did, I got my mouth washed out with soap.

I'm not joking. If I said something I shouldn't have, Mom gave me a warning that went something like this: "If you want to say that word one more time, then you know the consequences."

I'd say I was sorry and promise to do better. A half hour later, though, I'd be arguing with Chance over sharing our toys and forget and slip up and say something like, "Give me my Transformer, you moron!"

Then Mom would grab me and march me to our bathroom.

"Stick out your tongue," she'd say.

I'd always beg her not to do it, but she never backed down. Once I stuck out my tongue, she would rub a wet bar of soap all across it. Then I could wash out my mouth with water.

The soap tasted disgusting, and it made me angry the rest of the day.

When I got too old for the infamous soap-washing, she read

me scriptures like Proverbs 21:23: "Those who guard their mouths and their tongues keep themselves from calamity." She would also remind me of James 3, which tells us that the tongue is a small part of the body that likes to make great boasts. Just as a tiny spark can start a great forest fire, she said, the tongue can set your whole life on fire if you don't control it.

"With the tongue we praise our Lord and Father, and with it we curse human beings, who have been made in God's likeness," she read from James 3. "Out of the same mouth come praise and cursing. My brothers and sisters, this should not be. Can both fresh water and salt water flow from the same spring?"

That was a good question—and part of my education. I vowed to myself I wouldn't say anything I couldn't say if GranJan was in the room.

Years later something happened to me during my first season at Texas. I quickly discovered that ABC, CBS, and ESPN cameras followed the quarterback everywhere—and *I* was the quarterback. Not only did the cameras record my every step, but boom microphones captured my every word, or so it seemed, whether I was on or off the field. It was a bit disconcerting to learn that one stray word could be broadcast coast to coast on live TV.

After one game midway through my redshirt freshman year, GranJan gave me a call. "You know, Colt, I'm just really proud that you're not using some of the language those other boys use. I watch the games closely on TV, and I'm just so thankful that you don't say anything you shouldn't say. You don't realize how many young boys look up to you and appreciate that. I just want to tell you how proud I am that you don't use those words."

I gulped. In the back of my mind, I was thinking, *Man, GranJan has busted me. I've used some of those cuss words before, and I know I shouldn't.*

Back in high school, I went through a stage where I thought it was cool to throw in a cuss word here and there—just like my buddies did. There was certainly peer pressure to do what everyone else was doing, and I gave in to that part of it.

As I got older and matured some, I dialed the bad language back. In fact, I have trained myself not to use or rely on cuss words to make my point or to be more "descriptive" in my speech. But I can't say that everything that has come out of my mouth has been perfect, especially in the heat of competition—like in a football game. I'm an intense competitor and a fiery guy, and sometimes when I get angry or something goes wrong on the field, like when I throw an interception, the wrong words come out. I hate it when that happens, but it shows me that I continually have to work on my discipline and self-control.

So yes, I have said some choice words that I shouldn't say or don't *want* to say. Will that happen in the future? I'm afraid so because I'm not perfect.

In this area of my life, I ask God for grace.

At the same time, swearing is not part of my everyday speech, and as I've matured, I've found it a lot easier to control my tongue. All in all, I think I'm doing a good job there. I'm well aware that the cameras and microphones are on me from the moment I put on a uniform and step onto the field until I leave the stadium. Because of that, I strive not to say anything or act in a way that would misrepresent my name or my family or my team or my God.

Thank goodness I'm too old to have my mouth washed out with soap.

CHAPTER 4

Notes on the Bathroom Mirror

Colt

My parents were always looking for ways to teach me valuable lessons, although I sometimes may not have been too happy about it. Another lesson they impressed on me took place at the County Rodeo in San Saba when I was six years old.

Even today the annual summer rodeo is a big deal in small Texas towns. At that time, the San Saba County Rodeo had been going on for more than fifty years. Every summer the townspeople filled the grandstands to watch bareback riding, saddle bronc riding, bull riding, tie-down roping, mutton busting, and barrel racing. Oh, and the rodeo clowns and the pecan sack race were a lot of fun, too. (San Saba is billed as the "Pecan Capital of the World.")

That summer all my friends had been talking about the kids' steer riding contest. The winner received a shiny belt buckle, and the more I heard about the contest, the more I wanted to sign up. At the dinner table the night before the rodeo, I asked Dad if I could do just that.

Dad looked at me for a long time, which I knew meant he didn't think it was a good idea. "No, I don't want you to ride steers," he finally answered. "You could get thrown to the ground and get hurt."

"But Dad," I pleaded, "I promise I'm not going to get hurt."

Dad had his answer to my plea at the ready: "Son, those steers are big, powerful animals. You're just a little guy. Maybe when you get bigger."

I would not be deterred though. I uttered another appeal: "Dad, I can do it. I really can. You'll see."

Dad looked at Mom, and when I saw the raised eyebrows between the two, I sensed that Mom was on my side.

"Brad, perhaps he could—" and that was all Dad needed to hear.

"Okay, here's the deal," he said. "You can sign up. But when you put your name on that list saying you're going to ride, then you're going to ride. You can't back out."

I smiled and answered, "That's fine with me, Dad. I want to win the belt buckle."

The next day, Mom took me to the rodeo grounds, and I registered for the kids' steer riding contest, which was divided into age groups. I was in the youngest class of riders—the one for six-, seven-, and eight-year-olds.

As I registered, I learned there would be a round of competition on Friday night, and then the top three finishers would compete Saturday night for the first-place prize.

Come Friday night, I put on a white T-shirt, blue jeans, and cowboy boots. I loved the rodeo, and back then jeans and cowboy boots were my favorite things to wear.

My parents accompanied me to the steer riding contest and wished me the best before they returned to their grandstand seats. About twenty kids had signed up in my age group. We must have been quite a sight as we lined up for our chance to ride one of those big ol' steers—at least they sure looked big to my six-year-old eyes.

I can still remember the excitement I felt as I climbed the fence and dropped myself into the bucking chute. One of the rodeo hands helped me onto the back of the steer and instructed me to grab onto a rope with my right hand and keep my left hand in the air.

Before the guy could say, "Ride 'em, cowboy!" I was thrust out into the arena.

The steer gave me a bumpy ride, but I managed to hang on for eight seconds—which seemed like a lifetime. Then a couple of cowboys came to my rescue. I heard nice cheers, and my parents smiled widely for me as I exited the arena. When the first night of competition was over, I learned the exciting news: I was in the top three! I would be riding for the belt buckle on Saturday night.

When we came back that next evening, though, everything seemed different to me. This time the grandstands were filled; it seemed like everyone from San Saba *and* the surrounding county was there, including my friends from school. Not only was the crowd bigger, but so were the steers. They bucked and jumped in tight circles, and some of them seemed to have only one thing on their minds—physical revenge. I gasped each time a big steer tossed a rider to the ground.

I sat in the grandstands with my family, watching the competition. Then I leaned close to my mother. "Mom, I don't want to ride the steers tonight," I said.

Mom patted me on my forehead. "That's okay, honey," she said. "You don't have to ride if you don't want to."

I relaxed. I wasn't going to die that night after all.

Then I heard my father tell Mom, "Well, no, he *does* have to ride. He signed up to do this, so he needs to follow through on that commitment."

"Brad," Mom protested, "he doesn't have to ride if he doesn't want to. It's dangerous out there."

My father's face tightened into a mask. "You're right," Dad answered, "he might get hurt. But he signed up, and he's going to do it. He can't back out now."

Sniffling, I pleaded my case. "Don't make me ride, Dad," I said.

"I really don't want to go!" But my father wasn't budging.

I started to throw a little fit when the announcer said it was time for all the kids in the steer riding competition to get ready to ride. When Dad heard the announcement, he reached for my right hand and declared that we were going.

"Please, Daddy, please don't make me do this!" I squawked as he forcibly led me down the grandstand steps.

Brad

You should have seen the horrified looks I got from our friends and neighbors who watched the scene unfold. But I was committed, even though every mother in San Saba County thought I was a lock to win the "Worst Dad of the Year" award. Everyone knew I was the high school football coach, and I'm sure some of them were thinking, *The only thing that matters to him is winning. He'd even sacrifice his own son to bring home a trophy. That's the sorriest human being I've ever seen.*

I dragged a kicking-and-screaming Colt to the bucking chute. I lifted him over the rail and onto the steer, and I practically had to tie his hand onto that energetic steer, which was snorting and pawing in anticipation of being released into the arena. I'm sure at least some of the cowboys thought, *Coach McCoy, you've lost your mind.*

Colt

The gate swung open, and everything that happened after that was a blur. I'm told the wily old steer bucked like a banshee. Within seconds, it bucked me off, and I landed in front of the kicking animal. I busted my lip when I hit the ground, and before the cowboys could wave the steer away from me, it stepped on my back.

When I pulled myself to my feet, I heard loud cheers from the grandstand, but I was still fighting back tears. A half hour later, those tears turned to smiles, however, when I learned I had won first place as well as the prized belt buckle. I don't know why the judges thought I was the best steer rider that night—maybe I had stayed on longer than I had thought.

A few days later, after the dust had settled, I actually *thanked* Dad for making me ride that steer. I also told him how scared I was to ride that night, and then we talked about how you sometimes have to do things even when you're scared.

By making me ride that evening, Dad helped me learn two important lessons:

1. **You always finish what you start.** You never do something halfway, and you never quit until you've finished. Dad later told me he thought the steer riding competition would teach me a valuable lesson about not backing out of something after I had made a commitment, even though we both knew that would have been the easier path.

2. **Trust the advice of those more experienced than you.** On the first night of the steer riding competition, the rodeo organizers picked one steer for the kids in my age group, and off we rode. On Saturday night, though, they gave us kids a choice: we could ride a big steer or a smaller one.

Before the rodeo started on Saturday night, Dad and I visited the pen where they kept the two steers. "You're going to want to pick the bigger steer," Dad said. "The biggest one will be the easiest one to ride."

"Dad, I rode a big steer last night. I want to ride a smaller steer. I want to pick the smallest one because that will be the easiest one."

"I'm not so sure that's what you want to do, son. The smaller one will be the quickest and the fastest. You could get bucked off and hurt."

"No, Dad, you're wrong. I rode the big one last night, and the smaller one will be easier."

Dad let me have my way. "Fine," he said. "You're the one riding, so you can pick whatever steer you want."

So I picked the smallest one.

I got the ride of my life when that gate opened Saturday night. Up and down, up and down, and then I fell to the ground. It turned out that Dad knew what he was talking about. The smaller steer really *was* quicker and more agile than a bigger, lumbering animal.

I remember well how Dad came running out to the arena to help rescue me after I hit the ground. After he dusted me off, he gave me a big hug. As I wiped away the tears, I knew I had learned some important lessons about life that night.

That was my dad—preparing me for the path, not the path for me.

Brad

I think I slept on the couch for a week after that year's San Saba Rodeo.

But when Colt signed up for that kids' steer riding contest, I had a feeling he would change his mind about riding after seeing how big those animals were and watching his chums bucked off.

I wanted to teach Colt that you don't back out of your commitments. I wanted him to understand that no matter how hard it is to follow through and no matter how scared you are, once you say you're going to do something, you do it.

Colt

My parents were very intentional about teaching us boys values like sticking to our commitments. But that was far from the only value they taught us.

Another biggie in the McCoy household was asking if we could be excused from the table after supper. We couldn't just leave the table when we wanted to go play before bedtime; we had to ask to be excused and then wait for the answer.

Sometimes Mom or Dad would excuse us right away, but sometimes we heard another response, like, "No, you have to eat a little bit more," or "You can leave when you finish your vegetables." Once we had eaten enough, one of them—usually Dad—would say, "Okay, you can be excused. Take your plate to the kitchen. Clean it up and put it in the dishwasher."

There were also occasions when Dad made another kind of announcement, usually just before Mom served up one of her delicious apple pies for dessert. About that time, he'd tell us, "Listen up, guys. Mom's tired, and she needs a break, so it's Kids' Night in the Kitchen." That meant my brothers and I had to clean up after supper. Our duties on those nights included washing the dirty dishes, pots, and pans and cleaning the kitchen table. As we got older, Kids' Night in the Kitchen happened probably two or three times a month.

Dad always made sure we treated Mom right. He always backed her up when she got after us for not picking up our toys or for leaving our bikes out in the rain. Dad usually did that when Mom wasn't around to hear. In other words, he never tried to earn brownie points with her by saying, "See, boys, you need to obey your mother" when she was within earshot. Instead, he instilled in us the idea that Mom was the only woman in our lives right now, and since she was our mom, we'd better treat her right.

Part of that was having good table manners and picking up after ourselves. If one of us complained about "Kids' Night in the Kitchen," he'd say something like, "No, that's not how we do it in this house. You're going to take your plates and put them in the dishwasher so your mom won't have to do it. She cooked this meal, so you shouldn't expect her to clean up after you."

Dad's overarching message was that Mom wasn't our slave and that she deserved respect—as well as a break from doing the dishes every now and then.

Mom was a great mother who constantly looked for ways to encourage us. Everything she did was with the intention of giving us order and providing structure in the home. She was very intentional about being a good mom, and one of the things she liked to do was leave encouraging notes on our bathroom mirror each morning. The note might contain an apt Bible verse, or it might be a simple reminder about an important test at school that day.

I can remember many mornings when I wiped the sleep from my eyes, stumbled into the bathroom, and looked at the mirror, where I would see in the upper left-hand corner a note from Mom, written with a red marker:

Big math test. You'll do great today!
Joshua 1:9: Be strong and courageous.

Mom often wrote down other Bible verses to think about, and they often involved watching what we said. She'd write scriptures like Psalm 34:13, which says, "Keep your tongue from evil and your lips from telling lies," or Proverbs 10:14, which teaches, "The wise store up knowledge, but the mouth of a fool invites ruin."

On Saturday mornings, Mom's notes would be a list of the chores we needed to get done that day, like cleaning up our rooms, raking up the leaves, mowing the lawn, or feeding the goats. Weekday notes might include reminders for a Little Dribblers basketball game after school.

Mom's bathroom-mirror messages were her way of communicating information as well as her expectations for how the day should go. There was nothing authoritarian in Mom's approach; she just wanted me and my brothers to be organized and ready for the day ahead.

Mom also liked to write encouraging or thoughtful notes on pieces of paper and slip them into our pants pockets, or write them on a paper napkin and tuck them into our brown-bag lunches.

What kinds of things did the notes say?

Things like "I love you. Have a great day" or "Be sure to listen to your teacher." I was always too embarrassed to let my classmates see the notes, but I knew they were reminders that Mom loved me and wanted me to become the best I could be.

Brad

I always admired how Debra got up early in the morning before the boys stirred and wrote a Bible verse and maybe some things they needed to accomplish that day on their bathroom mirror. More often than not, she also included a note of encouragement in my sack lunch. I also knew that whenever I took a change of clothes for a road game, I could expect to find a folded-up note stuffed into one of my pockets. Sometimes she'd stick a note in my truck's ashtray. (I never smoked, so she'd leave the ashtray a little open so I had a better chance of spotting her encouraging note.)

The things she wrote to me on game days always meant a great deal to me because she had been a talented athlete who understood what competition was all about. Here's something she might write before a Friday night football game:

I love you, and you're going to do great tonight.
Your kids are going to play hard for you.
You've prepared your kids better than anyone else.

I loved receiving those notes. They lifted my spirits and re-minded me that my role as a coach—as well as that of a father to our sons—impacted young lives far more than I would ever know.

Colt

Whether it was in writing notes, sharing scripture, or teaching manners, Mom and Dad were always intentional about every aspect of parenting. They wanted to prepare me and my brothers for the future the best way they knew how.

Their deliberate parenting started with sharing their faith in Christ and why they believed it was important to go to church as a family. Dad and Mom believed it was important for us to attend church regularly because that was a visible expression of our love and worship toward God. Also, gathering with other believers bore witness of our faith and trust in Christ, and it was a public acknowledgment that we were part of the body of Christ.

But my parents were always quick to add that going to church didn't make you a Christian any more than standing in a garage made you a car. They taught us that accepting Jesus as personal Savior and being baptized for the forgiveness of sins and the gift of the Holy Spirit was the key to eternal life. They also taught us that gathering with like-minded believers was one way to learn about the Bible's teachings, to build relationships with other church members, and to serve others inside and outside the church. When Christ was within us, they taught us, we could be a ray of light to others.

Wherever we lived, we joined the local Church of Christ con-gregation and participated in Sunday morning, Sunday evening, and Wednesday night services. We were in church so much grow-ing up that it seemed like it was our home away from home.

In terms of service at our church, my dad carried on the McCoy tradition: if there was a potluck or a church social event, the church leadership could count on us to show up early to set up tables or to stay afterward to clean up and put away chairs.

We always built our summers around traveling to a Christian family camp. By the time I started school, the Yosemite family encampment had closed down, but the Church of Christ had other Christian encampments, and we loved the atmosphere and fellowship found at them.

We started going to the Red River Encampment in Red River, New Mexico. That family camp started in 1987, a year after I was born. Around two thousand people usually showed up at the end of June for the four-day encampment, which was held in mountainous northern New Mexico at the base of the Red River Ski Area. Each year, the McCoy Family Singers were invited to sing, and back in elementary school, I didn't mind that Daddy Burl would invite me—the oldest grandchild—to come onstage so I could join in singing the last couple of numbers at the close of the program.

But please don't get the idea that all we did at this "church camp" was pray and fast and sing all day long. This was more like a family vacation with Daddy Burl, GranJan, and all my cousins in the cooler mountain air. Most of the time, we would chase each other, throw Frisbees around, check out the forest, play putt-putt golf, and fish. There was always something to explore, lots of hamburgers and hot dogs to eat, and s'mores to make and eat around the campfire. I was never bored.

I also liked to throw the football around at camp. There were always kids there who were close to my age, and I'd ask them if they wanted to play catch. We would spend hours playing a game in which I would throw the "long bomb" to a streaking receiver, and then I would run a pass route to catch his pass back to me.

Even then, I liked seeing the ball in the air.

Brad

We saw taking the kids to the Red River Encampment as part family vacation, part Vacation Bible School. The organizers always had lots of fun things for the kids to do while the parents listened to speakers or participated in various workshops. In fact, Debra and I spoke at the 2011 Red River Family Encampment on the topic of growing Christian champions. Returning to Red River was like old home week for us and brought back wonderful memories.

Colt

What happened during four days each year at Red River was a continuation of what happened year-round in the McCoy household: have fun, work hard, serve others, and learn about God.

Serving others, Mom and Dad told me, was the way to become a leader. And to become the best leader, I couldn't float through life, float through school, or float through sports.

This is what I remember my parents saying: *You're not going to coast through school and not make your best effort. You are going to work hard and do your best and be a leader. It's going to be difficult as well as challenging, but if you put the work in, you will succeed. You are going to play sports and work hard as well. You are going to prepare. Great leaders are always prepared for the path ahead of them.*

When you read those words, it might sound like Dad and Mom were top-down, authoritative personalities who kept their sons on a short leash. Nothing could be further from the truth. Their tone of voice was loving but matter-of-fact, and they let us know that they were going to be there for us every step of the way. This was the best way, they thought, to prepare us to grow up to be solid, productive, God-fearing young men.

Brad

Over the years, I've dealt with hundreds of parents who've come into my office to sit down and talk about their sons and their participation on the football team or other teams I have coached. I can always see them subconsciously trying to prepare the path for their child. It's like they've brought an imaginary pickax and shovel with them so they can break up all the big rocks and push them off the road. Then they go about filling in the holes and making the path smooth so their sons will have an easy time without any problems.

But what happens to those children when the parents aren't there and a boulder falls on that path—or something even more catastrophic happens? I've seen many athletes fall apart when they face adversity on the football field because they have never in their lives encountered a rough patch of road.

The ball can take crazy bounces, and lots of things can go wrong between the sidelines, but you can't give up because if you do, you've lost already. Sadly, too many kids have never learned how to overcome adversity. That's because their parents prepared the road for their children, not their children for the road.

As I raised Colt, I told him all along there would be times when I wouldn't or couldn't make things easier for him. But I also taught him to view times of adversity as opportunities to become a stronger leader and to figure out a way to overcome the setbacks.

Colt

When Dad and I speak in public about "preparing the child for the path, not the path for the child," I sometimes jokingly say, "I think my dad was one of those fathers who put rocks in my path on purpose." I'm kidding, sort of, but whenever there were opportunities to teach me a golden lesson—like the time I tried to get out of riding the buckin' steer at the San Saba Rodeo—Dad didn't pass up the chance to help me learn something valuable about myself or about life.

I also talk about how Dad and I developed our own little ritual back when I was in the first and second grades. When I didn't take the school bus and he'd drive me to school, we'd be talking as he pulled up to the student drop-off. Just before I got out of the car, he'd always remind me that he loved me and that I should do my best and be a leader at school that day.

He said those three things so often that we developed a little routine.

"Have a good day at school, Colt. I love you, and remember to do your best—"

Dad would pause, which was my cue.

"—and be a leader," I answered just before I stepped out of the car. And off I'd go with my heavy backpack into San Saba Elementary School.

My riding to school with Dad meant he had a captive audience, and he used those moments to teach me about decision-making, serving others, and being a leader. He told me that it says in Proverbs that every young man who listens to God will receive wisdom. When I asked him what wisdom was, he told me it was like having good sense to do the right thing.

Dad taught me that the Lord grants "good sense" to those who believe in Him, that He protects them and guards their pathways. He taught me that God shows us how to know right from wrong and how to make the right decision. Our lives are filled with joy when we make the right decisions in life because we have the good sense not to follow dark paths set before us but to follow the right path. Following the path God sets before us, Dad said, is always the way to go.

Those mini-Bible lessons made a big impression on me, and later on several dynamic and influential Bible teachers in church also made a difference in my life. They, along with my grandmother, influenced me to read the Bible and learn scripture.

From early in my life—I would say around third grade or so—I developed the habit of reading the Bible every night before I fell asleep. I usually read for five or ten minutes. While that may not sound like long, the wisdom of God's words was implanted in my heart at a young age.

So that's a short description of how Mom and Dad prepared me for the path—God's path—and to do my best and be a leader. They loved sports and wanted to share that love with me because one of the fun things in life is becoming the best you can be—in the classroom or on the athletic field.

You see, Dad and Mom had some definite ideas on my future in athletics.

CHAPTER 5

HUDDLING UP

Colt

My grandfather Burl McCoy remembers the time he and Gran-Jan pulled into our driveway on a cold, blustery Sunday afternoon in February. I was a fifth grader at the time, and they had driven up from the family ranch to visit us in Hamlin, about fifty miles northwest of Abilene.

It wasn't a good day to be outside, yet there I was in the driveway with a basketball in my chapped hands. Dad had placed a freestanding basketball standard next to the concrete pad, and I loved practicing by myself and playing imaginary games. My favorite was putting on a fancy move and then driving past a faked-out "defender" on my way for an unmolested lay-in. Other times I pulled up and took one of my trademark jumpers, swishing the ball through the net.

On this particular occasion, my grandparents greeted me as they exited the car, and then they hurried inside because of the cold. I kept practicing my dribbling and shooting skills. An hour later, I was still outside in the freezing air, pumping jumpers from different spots on the driveway, when Daddy Burl came out to check on me.

"Colt, show me what you're working on," he said. Daddy Burl had retired from coaching the Abilene Christian women's basketball team five years earlier, but even in his mid-sixties, my grandfather remained a student of the game.

"I saw Michael Jordan do this crossover move on TV," I said. "I'm working on it, and I'm going to have it in my game next year."

Daddy Burl says he remembers chuckling because it showed him I had made up my mind to add a Jordanesque crossover dribble move to my basketball repertoire, even if it meant staying outside in the cold until I got it down. I don't recall that incident, but my grandfather does, and he loves telling this story because he says it shows how determined I was to better myself, even at a young age.

Whatever sport I played in those days, I never thought practicing was drudgery. To me, practicing was *fun*, even though playing in organized games with my teammates was even more so. Ever since kindergarten, I had hung around football fields and field houses, so the world of athletic competition felt normal to me. Consequently, I loved sports and being part of a team. The camaraderie captivated me.

I think I learned that love of sports from my parents, which shouldn't come as a shock to anyone. Let's face it: *both* my parents were jocks growing up. (I hope that's okay to say about you, Mom.) When you add in the fact that both my parents were coaching high school sports when Mom became pregnant with me, you can see why athletics were important in our home.

Important but not paramount.

As for my athletic genes, Dad and Mom each played a sport at the collegiate level, so they were both well-coordinated. There's no doubt I inherited their athletic talent, but that's not why I became a professional football player. I think I got to where I am today because of what my parents taught me *off* the field about the value of hard work, being a leader, and looking out for others before looking out for myself.

So far I haven't talked much about playing sports before I started junior high school. That's because in elementary school, sports were just one piece of the family pie. Sure, sports activities were a key part of our lives, but we had a lot of other things going on. I've already told you about our busy church schedule on Sundays and Wednesdays, and how the rest of the week I tried to be a good student at school: complete all my homework, study hard, and get good grades. Playing sports had to fit into our busy schedule, and for the most part, they did.

The only organized sports I played before junior high were Little League baseball and Little Dribblers basketball. I really liked basketball—that's why I didn't mind practicing outside in the cold—and I played point guard. Winning was important to me, so I liked it that every basketball team I played on always won. I loved the taste of victory and hated the sour experience of losing. I had to win, and if I didn't win, I got angry.

One sport I didn't play in grammar school, at least at an organized level, was football. Sure, I played pickup games during Dad's high school practices, and I threw tons of spirals to my friends when we played. But I wasn't allowed to play Pop Warner football. That's because Dad was worried that someone would teach me the wrong fundamentals and that I'd learn bad habits.

Brad

Colt's right—no Pop Warner football for him. While there were great dads involved in coaching youth football where we lived, I had seen firsthand what could go wrong when inexperienced fathers tried their hand at coaching. Fundamentals of football are important for young kids, and if kids are taught the wrong fundamentals from the get-go, there's a lot to unlearn when they get to the high school level. So I decided that my boys were going to wait until the seventh grade to play football, when they could play on teams coached by people I had hired or was responsible for.

There was another reason for my caution: Colt was a gifted

athlete. Part of my job as a coach is spotting talent, and anyone with a coach's whistle around his neck could see that Colt was more talented athletically than his peers. I wasn't going to hand him over to just anyone.

I didn't make a big deal about Colt's athletic precociousness, however. He was blessed with tremendous hand-eye coordination and a great arm, and I let it go at that. When he pitched in Little League, everyone saw how hard he threw. When he stepped up to the plate, he was one of the best hitters on his team. When Colt took to the basketball court, he'd score 80 percent of his team's total points. When Colt entered the second grade, Debra and I decided to move him up so he could play against older kids in junior basketball.

My wife and I had other decisions to make, too, and they involved my livelihood. Believe it or not, being a high school football coach in football-crazy Texas—and it doesn't matter how big or how small the high school is—is a mini-version of the coaching carousel seen in professional and college football. In fact, I would argue that being a Texas high school football coach can be worse because it's *local*. It's one thing being a coach who has to deal with crazy NFL fans or boosters of a major college program, but it's quite another to deal with close friends, even friends at church, who are disappointed because their sons aren't getting as much playing time as they think they should.

So there's a bit of a musical chairs situation in Texas high school football.

At any rate, you've already read how the wheels were greased for my departure from San Saba High School. From there we moved on to Kermit, Texas (named for Kermit Roosevelt, son of U.S. president Theodore Roosevelt), where I coached the Class 3A Kermit High football team.

Kermit was located at the very tip of the southeast corner of Texas, which meant we were a good two hundred miles from family and our land interests outside of Abilene. Before my only season at Kermit High School was even over, Debra and I agreed that this was not the place we wanted to be. Fortunately, we had barely unpacked the moving boxes.

When the season finished, I immediately started looking for greener pastures. I learned that the athletic director and head football coaching position had opened up at Hamlin High School. Our move there certainly put us closer to the Abilene area, and I also liked that Hamlin had a great reputation as a proving ground for coaches. A lot of good coaches had gone on from Hamlin to prominent Texas high school programs.

Being a proving ground cut both ways, however. I soon discovered that the Hamlin parents' expectations were high, meaning the team had better win. While Debra and I met some great people and enjoyed our time there, I found Hamlin to be a tough place to coach.

During my third year at Hamlin, it dawned on Debra and me that Colt's junior high and pivotal high school years were right around the corner. Could we see ourselves staying at Hamlin for the next five years? And was this where we wanted Colt and his brothers to play football?

We put out some feelers and learned about a head coach opening at Jim Ned High School in Tuscola, a West Texas town only fifteen miles south of Abilene. Debra and I drove down with the kids to check things out, and I liked what I saw. Jim Ned High—named after a nineteenth-century Indian cavalry scout for the U.S. Army—looked like a sleeping giant. Lots of upside. The facilities were superb for a 2A school with a student enrollment of 325 kids. And the close geographical proximity to Abilene was a bonus.

A couple of weeks before the Jim Ned school board offered me the job, I found out that the school was hosting a Little Dribblers basketball tournament for sixth-grade teams. I thought this would be a good way to check out the school again, as well as the kids who would be Colt's teammates in future years if we came to Jim Ned. We had heard this class was filled with stud athletes.

I put together a sixth-grade team that included Colt and Chance, who was a fourth grader at the time and, along with Colt, one of the best players on the team. We drove to Tuscola on a Saturday, and our scrappy team clawed its way to the finals, where host Jim Ned waited to play us. From the opening tip, we discovered that they were as good as advertised. They had ten or twelve superior athletes, way more than we had. Colt scored about 40 points to keep us in the game, but we ended up losing in double overtime.

The narrow loss was Colt's only defeat in a Little Dribblers game. On the way home, after the initial disappointment wore off, Colt began thinking about how much he wanted to play with that group of sixth-grade athletes from Tuscola. "I think I could play with those kids," he said. "That would be a lot of fun."

First I had to get the Jim Ned job, which meant I would be the head coach of the football team *and* the athletic director. I had a good feeling that if I got the job, Colt would be surrounded by a talented group of kids who would excel and help make him successful.

Colt

Dad was offered the Jim Ned coaching job a month or so later, and he accepted. This meant my third move in five years. I didn't mind moving again though. While I never *wanted* to move, since moving meant leaving my friends, I was always okay once we settled into a new place. I knew we were moving because that meant Dad got a better coaching job.

My parents helped me understand that moving meant I could make new friends while still staying in touch with my old friends. But Dad and Mom also made it clear that this was what we were doing and this was where we were going. How I reacted was up to me. I could either like it or not, but how I felt wasn't going to change anything.

My dad started the job at Jim Ned in late spring of 1998, with about six weeks left in the school year. My parents decided my father would commute to Tuscola (pronounced TUSS-koh-lah) every day (and take me with him) until the whole family could move that summer. That way, I could get to know the sixth-grade boys in Tuscola instead of waiting until the start of seventh grade in August. (Football practice for the seventh-grade team started on the first day of school.) In addition, Dad wanted to hold a couple of spring football clinics for me and my new teammates.

Hamlin to Tuscola wasn't an easy commute—an hour and a half one way. Sometimes our days were so long that we stayed in Tuscola and slept in the field house, where there was a room with some couches to lay on. Other nights I slept at one of my new friends' houses. Sometimes we drove to my grandparents' home, which was about a half hour away, just outside of Abilene.

Tuscola was a cattle ranching and wheat farming community that dated back to the nineteenth-century cattle drives that were part of the Great Western Trail. Around seven hundred people lived within the town limits. Highway 83 ran north-south through an eight-block central district that was home to one bank, three churches, one restaurant (The Home Place, which was open Thursdays, Fridays, Saturdays, and Sundays), a funeral home, a volunteer fire department, an antique shop, and a florist shop. A five-story-tall water tower dominated the center of the town.

Tuscola wasn't even big enough for a stoplight. A blinking yellow light hung over the intersection of Highway 83 and Graham Street, where locals hung out at Lantrip's, a convenience store that doubled as the town café with its own grill.

Jim Ned High School and Middle School were located on the same campus, at the northwestern edge of Tuscola's central district. One thing I liked about the campus right away was the great athletic facilities. The grass football field looked perfect (artificial turf would come after my graduation), and the Jim Ned Stadium grandstand had room for twenty-five hundred people on the home side and a thousand on the visitors' side, which meant that the teams got a lot of support from locals and from those living in nearby towns like Ovalo, Lawn, Goldsboro, and Novice. (The school district comprised 380 square miles.)

The Jim Ned school board also offered Mom a position as a PE teacher at the elementary school—where Chance and Case would be attending—in nearby Lawn. Not only did that give us more income, but my brothers could ride to school with Mom in the morning. In the afternoon, Mom had to stay and finish her work, so my younger brothers would ride a school bus to Jim Ned High School and hang out at the football field or gym until practice was over.

We all liked Tuscola right away. Mom and Dad rented a home across the street from the football stadium, which meant we could invite our new friends to play in our huge backyard. Plus Dad had keys to the gym.

After a year in Tuscola, my parents felt settled enough to start shopping for a home. They found a neat house on a ten-acre parcel split off from a large ranch about six to seven miles from the school. The home had four bedrooms, which meant for the first time my brothers and I each got our own bedroom. No more gas attacks when doing my homework.

Our new home was close to Buffalo Gap, a town half the size of Tuscola and home to the Buffalo Gap Historic Village, a complex of nine rustic and historic structures. We still had a Tuscola address, however. What was most important to my parents, and to me, was that we lived in the country with plenty of elbow room. The Abilene State Park and a large Boy Scout camp called Camp Tonkawa were nearby.

Living on a ten-acre spread meant we could have some animals. At different times, we had cows and goats. I know city kids would tell us there was nothing to do, but we liked the peace and quiet and our own blanket of stars each night.

We weren't there long before Dad had us busy mowing the grass and picking up rocks in the pasture. There were plenty of weeds to pull, too, because Mom and Dad had planted a vegetable garden—squash, okra, beans, and peas. As the oldest, I was given the responsibility of feeding the cows and goats and making sure they got water. We also had a donkey named Taco.

I remember Dad saying one time, "If you don't feed and water the animals, if you don't make sure the fence is good, then you will lose the animals."

Sure enough, one night all the goats escaped. I'm not talking about three or four goats, either. I'm talking about all twenty of them, and what happened that one night turned out to be a real mess. Someone had left a gate open—I'm not blaming Chance at all—and each of our goats ran for freedom. We called the neighbors to see if they had seen any of the animals on their property, but they hadn't. That would have been too easy.

We mounted a search on Dad's four-wheel all-terrain vehicle and then branched out on foot. It seemed like we were out there half the night, getting scratched and beaten up by sagebrush and prickly bushes, but we didn't find those goats. Sometime around midnight, Dad announced that any more searching was futile and that we were done for the night. Back at the house, though, Dad set out a bucket of feed. Sure enough, all the goats came back the following morning.

Living on ten acres of land wasn't all work. My brothers and I had BB guns, which were fun to shoot aluminum cans, rabbits, and small birds with—even though the BBs didn't seriously injure the birds or animals most of the time.

I knew that all guns—even BB guns—were not toys and must be treated with respect. I'll never forget the time Dad drilled down that lesson.

I was ten years old, living in Hamlin, and Dad thought it was important that I become acquainted with the damage a gun could inflict. We walked into the country with Dad carrying a shotgun and me holding several paper plates. He made it a point to show me that he was walking with the gun unloaded, pointed toward the ground, and with the safety on.

"Son, I want to talk to you today about the importance and seriousness of handling a gun, taking care of a gun, and being responsible for a gun. Guns are *serious*. Guns are dangerous. This is not a BB gun. This is a serious gun."

Dad had my full attention.

"Here, I'll switch with you," he said. Dad handed me the single-barrel .20-gauge shotgun, and I handed him a paper plate, which he attached to a fence post.

He returned for the shotgun, which he loaded with a shell. Then he aimed and fired from a distance of 10 yards.

The booming blast shredded a big hole in the middle of the paper plate. Make that a massive hole. The wooden fence behind the plate was chewed up pretty good, too.

"This is what this kind of gun will do to an animal, to you, to whatever," my dad said. "That's why it's important that you understand what a gun can do. There are no shortcuts to safety."

I got the message loud and clear. I remember looking at what was left of that paper plate and thinking, *Good night! That could blow a hole right through you.*

"Want to give it a try?" my father asked, holding out the gun.

My heart skipped a beat. "Sure, Dad."

He tacked up another paper plate and then returned to where I was standing. He showed me how to load the shell into the shotgun, close the breech, and assume a proper stance—my left foot in front of my right. Then I pressed the stock of the shotgun against the pocket of my shoulder.

"You're going to get a pretty good kick when you fire," Dad said.

I had heard about the kickback from shotguns, and I wondered if I would ever be able to throw a football again.

"If you're ready, you can take off the safety."

I pressed the tiny button safety located in front of the trigger guard.

I leveled the barrel and took aim at the paper plate. I slowly squeezed the trigger . . . and was nearly blown over from the kickback. But my shot blasted the paper plate into smithereens!

Dad and I did more target practice with his .20 gauge. A few weekends later, he took me skeet shooting, and I shot at clay pigeons thrown into the air. Once I got the hang of skeet shooting (especially improving my aim), Dad took me out bird hunting whenever we had a long weekend at Daddy Burl's ranch.

The next gun Dad introduced me to was a Remington .243 rifle. As any hunter will tell you, a rifle is a lot different from a shotgun, and deer hunting is a lot different from bird hunting. But I had heard stories growing up about Daddy Burl and Dad's deer hunting expeditions, and I wanted to bag my own deer, too.

A few months before we moved to Tuscola, Dad took me to one of the family ranches in Brownwood (southeast of Abilene) for my first deer hunt. I was twelve years old at the time and had just finished a hunter's education class. I didn't have a hunting license, though, because a license isn't mandatory in Texas until age sixteen.

As we drove to the family ranch in Dad's pickup, he took me through the whole process. "We're not shooting these animals just to shoot them," he said. "If we happen to shoot a deer, we're going to take the meat, we're going to process it, and we're going to eat it. That's the reason we're hunting. We will appreciate the animal for providing food."

Dad further explained that you don't just shoot a deer and then leave it in the wild to die, nor do you shoot a deer for the trophy antlers. "Today, if we bag a deer, I will teach you how to field dress the animal and take the meat," he added.

We spent the night in an old hunting cabin that had electricity but no running water. (We had a windmill to generate water from our well.) Dad woke me up an hour before dawn for a little breakfast. This was in December, and the temperature was freezing outside.

We put on warm clothes, and then we donned our camouflage gear—cap, jacket, and pants—which upped my excitement level. I was going hunting for real!

Dad knew right where to go, which was a good thing since it was still dark out when we began our trek. I would get the first shot, he said, and if I was successful, we would be taking home only one deer that day. "We're hunting for sustenance, not sport," he reiterated.

We walked about a half mile to a spot that placed us 100 or 150 feet above an open field. Several large boulders formed a natural blind. We took spots between two big rocks and waited for the sun to come up. It was still dark, and I hadn't gotten much sleep the night before, so I nodded off.

Then Dad tapped my shoulder. "Colt, take a look."

I opened my eyes, and the pinks and blues of dawn were filling the eastern sky. We were mesmerized by the sight of several deer below, moving across the field perhaps 100 to 150 yards away.

We watched them walk by, impressed by the beauty of four bucks making their way past our blind. "We have to be careful about which one we kill," Dad whispered. "We don't want to kill any of the young ones. See the last one? He's more mature than the other bucks, probably somewhere between four and a half and five and a half years old. He's got an eight-point rack with a nice spread," he said, referring to the buck's antlers. "He's the one you want to go for."

My Remington rifle was loaded with three 130-grain bullets, so I quickly bolted one into the chamber and crouched next to the boulder, which was at chest height for me. I placed the rifle on the rock to steady myself—and my nerves. I was shivering with excitement.

"Take your time. They still don't know we're here," Dad said.

I peered through my scope and found the trailing buck. I lined up the crosshairs right behind his shoulder so that my shot would go through his heart and kill him instantly.

"When you're ready, slowly squeeze the trigger," Dad said.

The buck's shoulder remained in my crosshairs. Satisfied that I had him in my sights, I blew out a calming breath.

Steady . . . steady . . . I pulled the trigger, and the strong kick felt just like the kick from the .20 gauge shotgun. The buck immediately went down, and I don't know who was more excited—Dad or myself. He gave me a high five, and then we shared lots of "All rights!" and hugs. This was my first taste of buck fever, and I was shaking from the excitement—and the cold.

The other three deer scattered. There was no reason to take a second shot.

We made our way down to where the buck had fallen.

"Nice shot," my father said. "You hit him in the shoulder, just where I coached you to aim."

"What happens next?" I asked.

"We field dress it so the meat won't spoil."

I'll admit that it was a gory sight watching my father use his knife and make the initial cut into the deer's abdomen. After Dad removed the intestines and stomach, he let me continue. He showed me how to remove the rest of the bodily organs, including the heart, lungs, and liver.

"You didn't know you were going to get a science lesson today, did you?" my father said.

"No, I didn't," I replied.

When we were done field dressing the animal, we dragged the carcass to the nearest road and left it there. Then we walked back to the hunting cabin, where Dad had left the pickup. We drove back and loaded my first buck into the truck's bed.

"We're not done yet," Dad said. "Now we have to clean it."

Back at the cabin, there was a big oak tree that provided shade. "We've been hanging deer on this same tree for twenty-five years," Dad explained. "Let me show you how you clean a deer."

Dad tied a rope around the deer's rear feet and hung the carcass to a tree limb. Then he proceeded to skin the animal, taking the time to show me how to do it. Once we were finished skinning the deer, the next step was quartering the animal—cutting the carcass in four different parts—and taking each quarter to an outdoor table so we could cut off the meat, which we placed in ziplock bags. I watched Dad make the initial cuts, and then he showed me how to cut meat off the bones. The larger sections of meat became steaks; the smaller bits would be used for chili meat or breakfast-type sausage.

"Even these little bits of meat will be great for Mom's venison chili," Dad said.

Brad

Our first deer hunting trip was one of those teachable moments about how to stalk a deer and take the shot—and a memory a dad never forgets. Another thing about deer hunting is that it teaches you decision-making. *Should I pull the trigger or not? Can I make a clean and safe kill shot? Do I need to get closer?* Plus you have to learn to control your emotions because the excitement of the hunt can lead to hurried and poor decisions.

I was able to show Colt how things work and talk about how there were a lot of people in this world who are biased against hunting and zero in on the cruelty and other aspects. I said I was sensitive to that criticism, but at the same time, I told him that I was teaching him how to hunt and stalk a deer with this idea in mind: *If you had been born during the pioneer days, you could have survived. You could have lived off the land.*

Actually, Colt had already seen how we lived off the land. Debra was a good cook with venison, and she served a lot of chicken-fried venison steaks. On other occasions, she would fill a slow cooker with chunks of venison and fresh vegetables. In wintertime, she also made a delicious venison chili with beans grown from our garden. We didn't know it at the time, but we were eating "organic" long before it became the trendy thing it is today. Think about it: our meat came from field-raised and grass-fed deer, and our vegetables came from our garden, free of pesticides. We also slaughtered our own cows, which were pasture-raised.

Having a freezer full of venison and home-grown beef got us through some lean times when I was a young coach and Debra was staying home with the kids. When we were living on just my salary, hunting for deer was an important part of feeding the family. After Colt started hunting at the age of twelve, he saw how he had a part in putting meat on the table. He took a lot of pride in that and felt like he was part of something special.

After that initial experience, we probably hunted a half-dozen to a dozen times a year, much of that in December after the football season was over and a month after the start of deer season in November. It was always an escape for us, going out deer hunting and sitting in the blind, talking, and waiting. We didn't always kill a deer, and that was fine.

Some of those talks in a deer blind are things that will stay with me for a lifetime. I can remember having all three boys in a blind together at the same time. I don't recall that we ever killed anything when we were all together, but I wouldn't trade those times for any "trophy" I could have hanging on my wall.

After Colt left for the University of Texas, where he experienced success and notoriety, hunting became one of his ways to release the pressure valve and to get away from people, from phones, and from the limelight.

Looking back, I think I took Colt hunting at just the right time. He was twelve years old, on the cusp of adolescence. A lot of changes were ahead, from his physical maturation to his spiritual development.

Two things happened during this time that showed me he was willing to be his best and be a leader willing to serve God.

CHAPTER 6

BAPTISM BY
FIRE AND WATER

Colt

One summer weekend before the start of my seventh-grade year, Dad organized a football clinic at Jim Ned High. As part of the strength and conditioning presentation, a nutritionist challenged the players to live healthy lives. He said a good place to start would be cutting out all of our soft drinks.

"If you want to be a good athlete, stop drinking Coke and Pepsi," he said. "They have too much sugar, too many carbs, and they're plain unhealthy. When you drink a Coke, you should fill up your Coke can two times with water and drink that so you can wash the soft drink right out of you. But the easiest thing would be not drinking Cokes at all."

We were sitting cross-legged on the gym floor, listening to this guest speaker, when I lowered my eyes. I was killing Dr Peppers all the time. I loved Dr Pepper, which was practically the official soft drink of Texas. There were hot summer days when I easily drank a six-pack a day.

Over the next few days, I thought about what the nutritionist had said. His advice made sense to me. I had never felt good after drinking a sugary carbonated drink. I didn't feel like working out or playing sports with a Dr Pepper in my stomach. And all those nutritionless calories couldn't be doing my body any good.

The following weekend, we drove to Arkansas to see Mom's parents. We were on our way back to Tuscola when we stopped at an On the Border restaurant right outside the Six Flags Over Texas

101

amusement park, midway between Dallas and Fort Worth.

Dad was a big Dr Pepper fan, too, so when he ordered one, I asked the waitress for a Dr Pepper as well. So did my brothers. Nothing out of the ordinary about that. We always ordered soft drinks when we ate at a restaurant.

I knew something, however, as we sipped our Dr Peppers during the meal: this was going to be my last soft drink for a long, long time.

"That's it," I said, after I took my final sip. "I'm not drinking these anymore."

"What do you mean?" Dad asked.

"That was my last Dr Pepper. Mark it down. I'm not drinking them anymore."

Dad pressed me for the reason behind my change of heart, and I said that the health guy at the football clinic promised I would become a better athlete if I didn't drink soft drinks.

"He said drinks like Coke and Pepsi slow you down, and I don't want to be slowed down," I said earnestly.

My father smiled. "Good for you, Son."

I've followed through on that vow I made to myself and to my parents and haven't had any carbonated soft drinks since that day. As of this writing, I'm going on fourteen years without drinking a Dr Pepper or a Coke and any other carbonated soft drink. Instead of soft drinks, I drink a lot of water and juice and the occasional Gatorade and Powerade, but I'll only have one of these sport drinks if I'm working out and need the electrolytes.

When I played at the University of Texas, my teammates noticed that I never drank soft drinks, so several times practical jokesters tried to "spike" my water bottle by filling the plastic container with 7Up or Sprite, thinking the colorless drink would fool me. Sorry, guys. Didn't work. Even if I unwittingly took a sip of the soft drink, I spit it out.

Choosing to be intentional about what I drank *and* what I ate was all part of my plan to become the best athlete possible. (I'm not a big junk food eater, either.) When I made the decision to forgo soft drinks, seventh grade was coming up, and I was looking forward to playing organized football, with pads and helmets and referees, for the first time.

I knew what position I wanted to play: quarterback. I wanted the chance to make split-second decisions, deliver perfect throws to my receivers, and run for daylight when chased out of the pocket. I wanted to be the player responsible for leading my team to victory.

When I talked to Dad about my desire to play quarterback, he was all for it and didn't try to talk me into playing another position. He reminded me, though, that the quarterback shoulders the responsibility for whether the team wins or loses, and he asked me if I would be fine with that.

"Yes, I *want* the responsibility," I said.

Ever since I had started watching Dad's quarterbacks spearhead their teams to victory back when I was in kindergarten and first grade, I wanted a chance to do the same. I knew that meant extra work, extra preparation, and extra study, but I was willing to do whatever it took to be a quarterback.

Like the times when I would shoot hoops in our driveway and let my imagination roam, I also imagined what it would be like to play quarterback in high school—and beyond. I had this gut feeling this position could take me places. I wanted to get good enough to play football in college, like my father had, but I wanted to play for a bigger school than Abilene Christian University. *Maybe I can play for a Division I school like Texas or Texas Tech,* I thought. *And if I can play at a Texas school, maybe I can play for the Cowboys someday.*

Those were my dreams as I entered seventh grade. In the innocent eyes of a twelve-year-old, the sky was the limit.

Brad

I privately smiled when Colt said he wanted to become a quarterback. Of course, I was going to do everything I could to help make that possible.

My duties at Jim Ned included being the athletic director, which meant I spent much of my day overseeing *all* the coaches and athletes. I also thought it was important for me to help out with the junior high athletes so that those young, impressionable players could get to know me. Someday they would be in high school, and I wanted them to be comfortable with me.

The first day of school was the start of football practice for the seventh-grade team. The way things worked at Jim Ned, the seventh-grade team practiced at 7:00 each morning, and all the players signed up for first-period PE starting at 8:05, meaning they could practice nearly two hours before the start of their regular class day.

I hired various junior high coaches, and they were quality people. One day I approached our seventh-grade head coach and told him, "Hey, I'm going to be here every day for you. I want to work with the quarterbacks because that's what I like to do, but it's your team. You'll call the plays unless I decide I want to. That is nothing against you, so don't get your feelings hurt. We'll do good."

The seventh-grade head coach understood my reasoning—that I wanted to shepherd my son's development as a football player as well as get the overall program aligned in the same positive direction, from the seventh grade to the twelfth grade. As it turned out, it was a win-win arrangement for everyone: our seventh-grade coaching staff got some extra help, and I got to work with Colt at a key time in his development.

I didn't just work with my son but with all his teammates, too. I was able to get most of my high school coaches assigned to junior high athletics, so we were all able to help grow these young athletes.

The junior high football team played its games on Thursday afternoons. Seventh-grade football can be described as a little boring and sometimes ragtag and sloppy, but this team was nothing like that. The boys averaged 40 points a game on offense and allowed just *one* touchdown on defense all season. Yes, this meant Colt's team was undefeated over a nine-game schedule.

In Colt's very first game as a seventh grader, I saw a glimpse of what he could do. On one play, Colt was flushed out of the pocket and ran to his right. He saw his receiver cutting across the field, hand up, signaling that he was open. Colt—running at full speed to avoid the rush—threw a frozen rope 35 yards downfield and hit his wideout between the numbers. That's when the light went on for me.

After Colt's third game that year, a father from the opposing team told me that Colt would one day win the Heisman Trophy, the honor given to college football's most outstanding player.

I put my hand on his shoulder and told him he was crazy.

Colt's eighth-grade team went undefeated, too, beating every 2A eighth-grade team on its nine-game schedule. Several kids in Colt's class were developing into special players, and they were becoming great friends who supported each other. I loved being around them all and continued to work as the quarterbacks' coach so I could keep a close eye on Colt.

When Colt moved over to the Jim Ned High School campus for his freshman year, I heard calls that I should bring him up to the varsity. I didn't think that was such a good idea though. For one thing, although Colt was growing, he hadn't yet gone through his major growth spurt, so he would have been at a physical disadvantage playing against juniors and seniors. Plus, I already had a good quarterback, Cody Lester, coming back for his senior year.

Cody was a great kid, and his parents are still good friends of mine. They had three sons, just like we did, and they all attended Jim Ned High School. Cody was a tremendous leader who commanded the respect of the kids and the coaches. He'd played well for us his junior year, and my thinking was that Cody would again do a great job for us while Colt developed with his peers on the junior varsity team.

In addition, we had a tremendous freshman class that included many of same kids who played against Colt in the sixth-grade Little Dribblers basketball tournament, and I wanted to keep those kids together. If I had plucked Colt and two or three other players off the junior varsity team and brought them up to varsity, the JV team would have suffered.

As it turned out, the JV team—with Colt calling the signals—went undefeated. When their season ended, I brought up Colt and several other players to help us during our state playoff run. Colt saw some action, which gave him a taste of what high school varsity football would be like.

Colt

When my freshman season of football was over, I moved right into basketball, even though the team had already been practicing for a month. I really enjoyed playing basketball. I liked the passing and the teamwork involved in the game, and I liked seeing the ball swish through the net. In one summer league game, I took seven straight three-point attempts from beyond the arc and made them all.

I played basketball all four years at Jim Ned, and I guess my claim to fame was hitting a 90-foot shot right at the halftime buzzer of one game. I had taken an inbound pass just inside the baseline, but there were only two seconds left in the half. I was way too far away from our basket to shoot the ball with two hands. It was a free shot anyway, so I put the basketball in my right hand and threw the ball like it was a long bomb pass on the gridiron. The basketball nearly struck the gym ceiling before zipping through the hoop. The ball was traveling so fast that it nearly tore off the net.

Our home crowd exploded. The two officials glanced at each other with a look that said, *What was that?* Finally, one of them said, "It's gotta be a three" and lifted both arms up—like a football official signaling a touchdown—confirming that I had released the shot before the halftime buzzer. The crowd continued to go crazy as I turned and jogged toward the dressing room for halftime.

Once my freshman basketball season was over, I wanted to play a spring sport, but Dad wasn't keen on me playing baseball. He told me that life sometimes requires you to make hard choices, and one of those hard choices would be not playing baseball.

Even though I would have enjoyed playing with some of my friends who were on the team, baseball was a little slow for me. I think it would have been okay if I could have just pitched, but I found out that if you were going to be a great baseball player, then you had to play all summer long, something my brothers and I did when we were young. But we also loved to go camping and fishing in the summertime, and I wouldn't get to do those things if I played baseball. It was an easy choice not to play high school baseball, especially since I loved football and basketball so much.

Since Dad thought I had a future playing quarterback, he said the other sports I played should complement what I was trying to accomplish in football. Basketball was an example of a team sport that helped football players with its emphasis on footwork and hand-eye coordination, such as shooting a basketball through the hoop. Conditioning and running are also a big part of the game.

Dad did urge me to run track during the spring sports season, no doubt thinking that running track would make me faster on the football field. There weren't that many track meets, which meant I had time to participate in spring football practice.

When my father talked up track, he undoubtedly thought of the stories of his father becoming a star hurdler in his college days. I said that running on the track team sounded fine to me, and in honor of my Daddy Burl, I chose hurdles. I ran the 110 hurdles, the 300 intermediate hurdles, and the relay events.

But then I heard that our golf team was a man short to play team matches. In high school golf, you need five players to field a team. I wanted to give it a try. I had never played before, but trying out new sports is something you do when you're a high school freshman, right?

Dad wasn't a golfer and definitely not the country club type. When I asked him if I could play on the golf team, he didn't like the idea that much because he couldn't see how golf could do anything for me athletically. He relented, however, because—as the athletic director—he knew Jim Ned wasn't going to field a golf team if I didn't play. He also thought golf might help me develop some positive mental qualities, such as perseverance.

Somebody had given Dad a set of old clubs, which he had stashed in the garage. Those old clubs were rusty and the grips were horrible, but I took them over to the golf course in Abilene (there was no golf course in Tuscola) and started teaching myself how to play.

I was surprised how difficult it was to hit a small white ball sitting motionless on a tee, but I kept beating range balls until I could get something going. I played horribly my freshman year, but by my junior and senior years, I was shooting in the 90s in 18-hole tournaments. (Today I'm a certifiable golf nut and play every chance I get, playing to a pretty solid 12 handicap.)

Juggling two spring sports wasn't the easiest thing to do, along with continuing my weight training for football. There were times when I'd get out of school to play in a 9:00 a.m. golf tournament in Abilene, then head back to Tuscola for an afternoon track meet.

I loved it though. Daddy Burl got a kick out of seeing me run his old events, and I loved having him come to my track meets. He remained a huge influence in my life, which is why I asked him to baptize me after my freshman year of high school. I had come to a point in my spiritual life where I wanted to make a public confession that I believed in Jesus Christ as my Lord and Savior. I believe that baptism is an act of obedience to Christ, an illustration of His death, burial, and resurrection, and a proclamation of my desire to follow Him.

That summer, while I was attending the annual Christian family encampment at Red River in New Mexico, I heard one of the youth speakers talk about the importance of baptism. Hearing him speak was an emotional experience for me, and I wanted my baptism to be a special time for my family.

In my fourteen-year-old mind, there could be nothing more special than having my Daddy Burl baptize me. But I didn't want to slight my father, who was *the* great spiritual teacher in my life. One day I talked to him about it as we rode around in his truck: "Dad, I would love for you to do it, but I think it would be awesome if Daddy Burl could baptize me."

My dad smiled. "I think that would be awesome, too," he said.

My grandfather was quite moved when I asked him to baptize me, and we set a date and a place—July 8, 2001, at Oldham Lane

Church of Christ, our home church in Abilene, which had a baptistery behind the pulpit.

I wore a white robe and Daddy Burl wore chest-high fishing
waders as we stepped into the baptistery, filled with water three
feet deep. As we prepared for my baptism, Daddy Burl became
so emotional that he had trouble talking. After gathering himself,
he spoke to me about the seriousness of what I was doing and the
importance of staying faithful to the Lord.

Then he reached forward and placed one of his strong arms
behind my back. Before he lowered me into the water, he said, "I
baptize you in the name of the Father, the Son, and the Holy Spirit
for the forgiveness of your sins." And with that, I got a dunking.

I popped back up to the surface to the applause and singing of
the full Sunday morning church congregation.

The Bible says that when John the Baptist baptized Jesus, a
voice from heaven announced in a loud voice, "This is my beloved
Son, in whom I am well pleased."

It was my prayer that my life from that day forward would be
pleasing to the Lord.

CHAPTER 7

THE JIM NED YEARS

Brad

There's an old saying in the coaching business that goes like this: "His players will run through a wall for him."

I have always tried to be just that type of inspirational coach for my players, and in order to get players to go beyond what they thought they were capable of, I put a lot of emphasis on the relationship part of coaching. I got close to my kids, made them feel important, and constantly stressed the value of teamwork. When they saw my passion for preparing them to play their very best, most of them bought into the program, as another old saying goes.

Sure, I had a goal of winning games and championships, and many years we accomplished those goals. But at the same time, I knew high school football was the end of the line for 99 percent of my players, as far as organized ball is concerned. That's why I've always viewed football as a vehicle to prepare young men for a life of character. I wanted to help them to someday become better men, better businessmen, better husbands, better fathers, and better church leaders.

To instill the kind of discipline I knew my players needed, I instituted a team curfew and team training rules. The players knew there would be consequences when they broke team rules. Some years I had to discipline far more players than I wanted to, but I like to think that they are better people today because they accepted my coaching methods and my rules.

At the same time, I knew I had to walk the talk with the kids, just as I had to do with Colt and his brothers back home. Coaches are role models, and kids have an uncanny way of seeing right through you if you say one thing but do something else. I held myself accountable as well; I've always believed that if I gave my kids a set of expectations that I couldn't live up to, then I needed to find another line of work.

I share all this because when Colt became a sophomore and was ready to start his varsity football career at Jim Ned High School, I faced a coaching challenge: I was the head coach and my son wanted to play quarterback. Everyone in town knew this dynamic, and I'm sure that even though Colt was 28–0 in sub-varsity games, they gossiped over at Lantrip's about whether I would name him as my starter.

I had never faced this situation before, but I knew one thing: I couldn't hand Colt the starting quarterback position on a silver platter. I decided to take myself out of the equation. During the start of two-a-day practices, I asked my assistant coaches to make the final decision on whether Colt would be our starting quarterback. In other words, I recused myself. I didn't want anybody in Tuscola or the Jim Ned family to think that just because Brad McCoy was the head coach of the football team, Colt McCoy would automatically be named the starting quarterback.

Colt

I knew going into my sophomore year that I had to work for the starting role. My thinking at the time was that I had to work twice as hard as anyone else and prove that I was ten times better than my competition.

I didn't receive a free pass. In some ways, my father made things even tougher on me. But he had never been one to prepare the path for me. In fact, he tossed a few more rocks in my path.

Let me give you an example.

If I threw an interception in practice, turned the wrong way to hand off, or held the ball too long and got sacked, Dad yelled at me more than anyone else. I don't mean the type of yelling where you could see Dad's vocal cords straining in his neck. I'm talking about the typical coach's yell—except I was verbally reprimanded in a tone more intense than what other players received.

Since I was the only player who rode home with the coach and ate dinner with him, I asked him one time why he was singling me out. "Did I screw up that bad today?" I asked. "Or did you feel that you needed to make an example out of me?"

My father sighed. "Yes, it was one of those times I thought I should make an example of you. I have to make sure that everybody knows that if I—the coach—can get on you, then I'm not playing any favorites."

Brad

The hardest part of coaching Colt was trying to find a balance between nurturing and correcting. I can assure you that playing the games on Friday night was the easy part.

If one of our defensive backs made a great play in practice and intercepted one of Colt's passes, I let it go. But I sometimes had to make an issue about the decision-making part of Colt's game—like when he made a throw he had no business trying. On those few occasions when he made dumb mistakes, I was tougher on him.

Those misfires were few and far between. You see, Colt had always been a fast learner, and he usually didn't make the same mistake twice. As a coach, it was like this: if he made a bad throw into coverage, then I almost felt like I *had* to take advantage of this scarce opportunity to coach him hard in front of his teammates. With Colt, there weren't many occasions to do so.

I remember a day when several of his teammates approached

me after practice and told me they were concerned because they thought I had gotten on my son's case a bit too much. "Coach, you were too hard on Colt today," said one of the boys.

I listened. After a moment, I remarked that I appreciated their courage in speaking up, and I promised to take to heart what they said. Colt's friends left knowing that Coach McCoy's expectations for Colt were really high. At the same time, I reminded myself to make sure Colt always knew, when push came to shove, that no matter what I said or how I reacted to him on the practice field, I loved him unconditionally. I made sure I reminded him that anything I said in a coaching context was for his best interests. I knew I could do that with him because we had forged that kind of a relationship long before the competitive times.

Thankfully, that wasn't difficult to do because Colt was largely self-driven. I never had to push him or be a "football dad." For example, we'd be sitting at the dinner table, and he'd say things like this:

- "I want to be the best I can be. Can you help me?"
- "I want to play in the biggest college I can. What do I have to do to get better?"
- "I want to get to the NFL someday. Do you think that's possible?"

Whenever the discussions veered in this direction, I reminded him, "You are going to have to work with whatever body God gives you. Yes, you have ability, but in the world you want to play in, there will be hundreds, if not thousands, with the same goal. There has to be a difference maker, something about you that defines greatness because you'll be competing against guys bigger, stronger, and faster than you. You will have to flat-out work harder to be better than them."

Colt

What was going to be the difference maker? It would have to be the way I trained and the amount of practice I put in. And if I strived to work harder than everyone else, it stood to reason that I needed more rest than anyone else.

I read where sleep was especially nourishing for teen boys because sleep releases certain hormones that stimulate growth and repair damaged tissue. The more one sleeps deeply, the more growth hormones are released into the body's bloodstream. I had never been a night owl anyway—we generally awoke bright and early in the McCoy family—but I knew I would have to guard my sleeping schedule at a time when my friends were staying out later than they did in middle school.

During my high school years, it was rare to catch me awake after 9:30 on a school night. When I began my freshman year, Mom and Dad gave me a midnight curfew on weekends (my parents and grandparents always told me that nothing good ever happened after midnight), but you could count the number of times I stayed out that late on two hands. Going to bed early was a decision I made, and my friends quickly learned that if they invited me to go out to the movies in Abilene, then we'd better go to the 7 o'clock show or it wasn't going to happen.

I was never a big party guy. Sure, I liked to hang out with friends, but I never liked to stay out late. Nor was I going to drink alcohol. I didn't judge anybody, didn't condemn anybody, but my friends and classmates knew I wasn't going to drink and go crazy. When someone threw a big party on a Saturday night and I knew drinking would be going on, I didn't show up. Instead, I would find a close friend or two and persuade them not to go to the party but to hang out with me instead. That number of friends would grow as time went on.

This didn't stop me from being involved in school or striving to be a leader. Sure, the parties happened, but it got to the point where I wasn't even asked to drink anymore. It wasn't a big deal; everyone respected who I was.

Brad

Colt made the decision himself that he wasn't going to drink, but quite honestly, I heard parents whisper, *No one does this on his own . . . . He is a mean dad . . . . There's no way he should shelter his child like that.*

Hearing that stuff was rough on Debra and me. We took a lot of shots for supposedly being parents who pushed our kid into doing things he didn't want to do—or kept him away from some things he *did* want to do. But it was Colt who made the commitment to become the best person, the best student, and the best quarterback possible, and that meant staying completely away from alcohol. He had a resolve that could not be shaken, and that desire came all from within him.

I could see that fire burning within him to be the best. When he asked me for my help, I committed myself to helping him get better as a player and a person while he was under our roof during the pivotal high school years.

I also tried to keep Colt grounded with tangible reminders that in this thing called life, it's not all about him. For example, we had a ministry at our church that helped out widows on Saturday mornings, and I suggested that Colt sign up to help out. He and several of his buddies from his youth group decided to take part in the ministry, and they were introduced to one widow who needed their help. They would show up at her house and mow her lawn, clean up her yard, take out her trash, sweep her porch—whatever needed to be done to spruce up her place.

On Sunday mornings before church, I would take Colt and the boys to a nursing home, where we would spend a half hour or so talking to elderly people, praying with them, and serving them communion. Then we would go to church as a family.

Colt

As much as I resisted doing stuff like that—there were other things I would rather have been doing on Sunday mornings than visiting a nursing home—I learned that it truly is more blessed to give than to receive. Dad and Mom were setting a foundation for a servant attitude that is very much part of my life today, and it went like this: *You will be a servant for the rest of your life. This is the kind of stuff you're going to do. God tells us in His Word that we are to take care of the widows, take care of the sick, feed the poor and hungry, and we've been blessed immeasurably with enough to eat. Service to others never goes out of fashion.*

So the idea of servant leadership was something being ingrained in me as I crossed over the breezeway between Jim Ned Middle School and Jim Ned High School. When I started high school, our youth group would visit a retirement home on Sunday nights once a month and share a devotional and lead the seniors in singing from the hymnal. For some reason, it seemed like I was always the one who led the singing. It might be because the guys in my youth group were too scared to sing—except for my cousin Jividen McCoy. I guess my experiences singing in public with the McCoy Family Singers were put to good use after all.

I couldn't wait for my first season of varsity football to start. I wore a red-and-white Jim Ned jersey with a No. 4, the same numeral as Brett Favre, the Green Bay Packers quarterback I looked up to. We started the season off great and kept winning. I was passing well and racking up lots of yards.

Then an interesting thing happened about midway through my sophomore season.

We had just beaten Coahoma High, and I'd had a good night. As I jogged off the field, several kids stopped me—I think they were coaches' kids from the other team—and thrust programs and a pen toward me.

"Can I have your autograph?" asked one youngster who looked to be around eight years old.

No one had ever asked me for an autograph before, and the request stunned me. I didn't even know how to do an autograph. I looked around and spotted Coach Lavallee, one of Dad's assistants. "What do I do?" I asked.

"Sign it," Coach Lavallee answered. "It'll probably be the first of many."

I shrugged and signed, careful to write "Colt McCoy" clearly. (Even today I try to sign my entire name legibly because GranJan said I should make sure that everyone can read my signature. I sometimes add "Col. 3:23" for Colossians 3:23, which is one of my favorite Bible verses. The verse is a great reminder to me of how to live life: "Whatever you do, work at it with all your heart, as working for the Lord, not for human masters.")

We won our first seven games, and waiting for us was Bangs High School, whose big weapon was a bruising 215-pound running back named Jacoby Jones, who loved to lower his shoulder and knock over players like bowling pins. (Jacoby would later go on to play football at Baylor University, the school my wife attended.)

I haven't mentioned this so far, but starting in the seventh grade, I always played *two* positions in football: quarterback on offense and free safety on defense. This is known in football as "going both ways," and playing every down is quite a load to carry. At small schools where the talent pool of players isn't that deep, the better athletes are asked to play offense and defense. (Oh, and did I tell you that I handled the punting duties as well?)

I played free safety during my sophomore year, and back in those days, I thought intercepting the ball was just as fun as completing a long post route. Well, on one play against Bangs, Jacoby Jones turned the corner and gathered steam as he ran up the field. I was one of the last Indians standing—we were known as the Jim Ned Indians—between Jacoby and the goal line. I instinctively threw my body in front of his thick legs, and I got kneed in the helmet. My head flew one way just as one our big defensive tackles dove into the pile and kneed me on the other side of the head. At least, that's what Dad told me had happened; I was knocked out on the play and don't remember a thing.

I'm told I looked like a newborn deer trying to get on his feet. I'd stand up, wobble, and then fall down. I'd try to get up again, only to tumble again to the ground.

"Are we going to GranJan's house now?" I asked. "When are we going to GranJan's?"

I was barely coherent. My eyes were open, but it was like I was not there at all.

Things happened in a hurry after that. I was rushed by ambulance to the emergency room, where I received medical attention. I later learned that I had suffered a concussion and was told not to play football for a month, meaning I was done for the rest of my sophomore season.

It was just as well. After losing that night to Bangs, we lost our next game, against Winters High, before finishing with a victory against Dad's old team, San Saba. Although we had an 8–2 record, we didn't get into the playoffs. I don't think my parents would have let me talk them into letting me play anyway.

Brad

Well, that one's on me. What can I say? I made sure Colt never played another down on defense. That's what you call being a smart coach.

Colt played very well his sophomore year, but we both knew his junior season would have a huge say in whether he would get the chance to play college ball. I knew something about the college recruiting process, and I was aware that major college programs zero in on the elite quarterbacks the summer before and during their junior years. That may sound unfair to late bloomers, but that's the way the system works.

If a player wants to become a college quarterback, then he must attend college football camps the summer before his junior year. That way he can make his name familiar to college coaching staffs. It's at these summer camps that players show college coaches what they can do. After that, a quarterback has to put up great numbers during his junior season so that college coaches will scout him. Performing well also gets high school players ranked on influential recruiting websites like Rivals.com, Scout.com, SuperPrep.com, and PrepStar.com.

Colt played at a 2A school with an enrollment of only 325 students, so it would be an uphill battle for him to get noticed. No one in the history of Jim Ned High football had ever gone on to play Division I football. Players from the smaller schools just don't get recruited, and because of that, I felt like we had to get him to the college football summer camps.

Colt

College football camps serve a dual purpose. Young players get a chance to throw and improve their skills under the eyes of experienced college coaches, and those same coaches take notes on players they'll recruit later.

In the spring of my sophomore year, Dad called the football offices at the University of Texas, Texas A&M, Texas Tech, Southern Methodist University, and Baylor to ask about their summer football camps. The coaches usually answered, "Sure, we'd like to have Colt come to our camp. Let us check him out. That will give us a baseline."

I was excited to hear that. I signed up for all five college camps, as well as the Nike Camp, an invitational camp held at Texas Christian University (TCU) that always drew a lot of coaches and scouts.

If I was going to play college football, I wanted to play somewhere in Texas so my family could come watch me play. I didn't have a particular favorite at the beginning of the recruiting process, even though I was an A&M fan growing up and often wore the Aggies' T-shirts and hats because I had family members with connections to the school. I also liked the University of Texas and Texas Tech. Most people in Tuscola seemed to be Texas Tech fans.

The camps at Texas A&M, Texas Tech, SMU, and Baylor, as well as the Nike Camp at TCU, went well for me, but I was really interested to see how my last summer camp—the one at the University of Texas—would go. The Longhorns were a powerhouse program, and Coach Mack Brown had put together some great teams since his arrival in 1998. During my freshman and sophomore years of high school, UT was one of the best college teams in the country, finishing in the top five in the Bowl Championship Series (BCS) standings with an 11–2 record both seasons.

The University of Texas football camp, held at one of the Longhorns' practice fields in Austin, was fairly typical of how these camps go. The minicamp lasted just one day, meaning I had a small window to make an impression. When I showed up at the practice field, there were two hundred to three hundred kids in attendance, and probably fifty of them were quarterbacks. We were split up according to our class: sophomores, juniors, and seniors. I was in the junior class. A couple of coaches watched us loosen up and throw the ball. They were looking at things like arm strength, size, and athleticism.

Then they had us throw to receivers running routes. With three dozen quarterbacks in my class, I didn't get many throws or much feedback from the coaches. The coaches weren't saying anything, so it was hard to get a feel for what they were thinking. That frustrated me. I thought I threw some good balls, but I had no idea where I stood when we were done at the end of the day.

Then it dawned on me: I was being ignored. I wasn't getting a look because I played for a 2A school.

Being overlooked at the UT camp didn't deter me from wanting to go to the University of Texas to play football. Just the opposite happened: everything I saw about the program that day impressed me and made me want to go to UT *even more*. The facilities were awesome, the school was top-notch, and the Longhorns were riding high as one of the best major college football programs in the country. I just wished they had taken a better look at what I could do.

On the drive back home, I turned to my dad and said, "I'm going to play at UT someday. That's where I'm going to go to school, and I'm going to be the quarterback there."

He gave me a long look.

"I know you don't think that," I continued. "You might think I didn't do that good today, but I'm just telling you, I'm going to be the quarterback at UT one day."

"I'm good with that." And that's all he said.

I turned the other direction and looked outside at the scenery along Highway 183. *I'm going to show them,* I thought. *They didn't want to talk to me. They didn't even want to look at me. I'll show them that they're going to want me. They will know that I'm going to be the quarterback there.*

This was the first gallon of kerosene poured on the fire in my gut to play college football at the University of Texas. I knew that if that was going to happen, then I had to play very well and lead our team to the state playoffs my junior year. I also knew we probably had to win the state championship because colleges don't often send their coaches out to scout 2A regular-season games.

I knew one other thing for certain: I had to get bigger and stronger. I was probably 6 feet tall at the time, but I was as skinny as a split rail. I barely weighed 170 pounds. To get bigger, I decided to work out at the Jim Ned weight room every morning at 5:30 throughout the rest of the summer, drinking protein shakes on the way to the gym. When school started in the fall, I kept working out before school. Then I had football practice every day from 3:00 to 5:30 p.m. Sometimes I'd lift again after practice before going home to eat Mom's great cooking, which gave my body the fuel it needed to grow bigger and stronger.

I gained between five and ten pounds of muscle between the UT football camp and the start of my junior year of high school football. That may not sound like much, but I noticed the extra strength when I threw the ball.

When my teammates noticed how much I was in the weight room, it inspired them to work harder during the off-season, too. Missing out on the playoffs the year before—even though we had an 8–2 record—lit a fire underneath all of us. We weren't going to allow anything or any team to derail us.

The effort was well worth it. What a special season in 2003! We kept winning, and I had a great time throwing tons of touchdown passes. We were the talk of Tuscola, and our fans knew they'd better show up before game time if they wanted a seat on our side of the field.

About halfway through the season, Dad started receiving phone calls from college coaches around Texas—and neighboring states—asking about me and wondering if he would send them game tapes. (The digital revolution was still a few years off.)

Then I noticed clusters of men I didn't recognize standing on the sidelines during our games. Most held clipboards and made notations. I knew most of the Jim Ned parents by sight, so I figured this could only mean one thing: college coaches were coming to my games.

When the University of Texas sent out one of its assistant coaches, Mike Tolleson, to take a look at me, my heart skipped a beat. Coach Tolleson's recruiting territory included Tuscola and the Abilene area.

Brad

The question I heard most from college coaches was this: "Do you think Colt can play at the next level?"

They asked that question even though they knew my response would be somewhat biased, which is why they also asked the other coaches on my staff, as well as opposing coaches, the same question.

I think people like Coach Tolleson saw two things about Colt:

First, his quiet leadership and lack of bravado or calling attention to himself.

Second, his rifle-like arm and pinpoint accuracy throwing the football.

Colt had a leadership style on the field that coaches love, and this isn't his father speaking. He was not a rah-rah guy who yelled and screamed at his teammates. He led by example, and coaches who have been in the business a long time picked up on that. Kids like Colt are so rare that when these coaches came across him, they became enamored with him. They couldn't keep their eyes off Colt because of the way the entire team followed him—not because he yelled at them but because he had the personality and mannerisms of a quarterback that other players want to play with. The college coaches saw that Colt's teammates didn't want to disappoint their quarterback, and they lifted their level of play in response.

Besides witnessing how he was a great leader of his team, the coaches and scouts saw something they didn't catch sight of very often: his accuracy throwing the ball.

When most quarterbacks, especially at the high school level, throw a football, there's a bit of a wobble on the ball that takes it off target. But when Colt threw, he delivered such a tight spiral that the football never deviated from its path. He was like a crossbow launching an arrow. Part of that was arm strength, part of that was practice, and part of that may have been the curved pinky finger on his right hand, which he broke in a game and which healed in a way that his pinky naturally followed the curve of the football. That allowed him a tighter grip.

"Watch when Colt throws the ball," I said to college coaches sitting in my office. "He doesn't miss. He will be on target and on the money every time." There were practices, I said, where the ball never touched the ground. "That's not all on Colt because his receivers have to be able to catch it, but he can put the ball in such a place that receivers have no problem catching it."

Here's an example of what I'm talking about. We were playing Clyde High School, and one of our receivers—Justin O'Dell, who stood around 5 feet, 8 inches tall—was having trouble getting separation from his defender. He kept getting held up at the line, which meant Colt couldn't throw to him.

My offensive coordinator, Jeff Williamson, got Colt and Justin together between offensive series and told our receiver he had to use a "swim technique" to get separation. This is where he places his left hand on the defender's shoulder and then uses his right arm to "swim" over the top and get away from him. Coach Williamson told Colt that as soon as Justin made separation, he had to get him the ball, since he'd be open for only a split second.

Our offense went out and ran the play. Justin used the swim technique, and the instant his arm came off the defender, Colt stuck the ball into the crook of his bent elbow. Justin kept running in full stride and scored a touchdown.

When Justin came back to the bench, Coach Williamson and I congratulated him for the great route and catch.

"I never saw the ball," he said, huffing from the exertion. "All I was thinking about was doing my swim. When I turned, the ball was stuck right in my arm. After that, I was gone."

Colt grinned at Coach Williamson. "Is that where you wanted the throw?"

Coach Williamson laughed because he knew my son was being facetious.

With Colt playing at such a high level, everything we touched seemed to turn to gold. Jim Ned went undefeated through the regular season, and then we kept winning in the state playoffs.

Colt

We went undefeated for our first fourteen games, which took us to the Texas State 2A championship game, held at Ennis High School, forty miles south of Dallas.

Jim Ned had never had a football team go this far in the state playoffs. It seemed like the entire town hung up a Closed sign and made the three-and-a-half hour drive to Ennis to support us. We were about as sky high as possible as we took the field against San

Augustine High, which had traveled just as far from a small East Texas town near the Louisiana border.

The playing conditions were challenging for the mid-December game—bitter cold temperatures in the twenties and a stiff north wind. We came out and scored first, but San Augustine tied the game 7–7 on a 60-yard pass play just before the half. That seemed to give San Augustine the momentum.

I had hurt my thumb in the first half when my hand hit a lineman's helmet, aggravating an injury I'd suffered earlier in the season. When we came out to play the second half, I couldn't grip the ball well or throw with the accuracy I wanted. The bitterly cold wind chill made things even worse. Meanwhile, San Augustine kept churning out yards with its ground game, keeping our offense off the field, which was really frustrating because we had been averaging 40 points a game.

Three long second-half San Augustine drives sealed our fate. As the seconds ticked off in a 28–7 defeat, I took a knee and shed a few tears. I desperately wanted to win that game, and as a seventeen-year-old quarterback playing for a state championship—and knowing this could be my only opportunity—our loss devastated me.

Brad

I found Colt at the 50-yard line, with tears in his eyes, looking very down on himself. My youngest son, Case, who was a sixth grader at the time, stood with me. He, too, was wiping away tears.

To be honest, I felt distraught as well. I had never seen my son so upset.

I reached down and gently pulled Colt to his feet. Then I put an arm around his shoulders. "C'mon, Colt. Let's go. Snap out of it. It's over. We gotta go."

He looked at me, and through a thin film of tears, he said, "You don't understand. I don't know how to do this. I've never been here before."

Colt lowered his head. "How . . . how?" he kept asking.

"I'm sorry, Colt. It hurts not to win the state championship, but you and your team played your hearts out. It wasn't meant to be."

"But Dad, this is the first time I've ever lost a football game."

What he said hit me like a thunderbolt. Colt was right. Ever since he started playing competitive football in the seventh grade, he had never been on the field at the end of a game that he lost. The previous year, Bangs High School's bruising runner Jacoby Jones had knocked him out, and he was taken for an ambulance ride before the end of the game. He hadn't played the following week against Winters, the only other game we lost.

I did the math. From the seventh grade all the way through his junior year, he had won fifty consecutive games.

Colt and I had some great conversations on the bus ride back to Tuscola and in the days that followed. We talked about how good life was and how sometimes things happen the way you expect them to but how sometimes they don't. We talked about Colt's leadership through winning and, yes, through losing.

Everything that happened in Ennis would help Colt handle life's inevitable disappointments in the future, I told him, but he could hold his head high. Sure, we had come up short in the state championship game, but we had been part of a special season.

Colt had done everything he could. He had thrown for fifty touchdowns in fifteen games, an average of more than three TD passes per game, a state record at the 2A level. He had passed for almost 4,000 yards and helped our offense score an incredible amount of points.

Colt McCoy looks downfield in his first NFL start, October 17, 2010
in Pittsburgh, Pennsylvania. Colt played well in "Blitzburgh," but
the Steelers won 28–10 to spoil his pro debut.

AP Photo/Gene J. Puskar

Colt, at four years of age, sports the uniform of the now-rival Dallas Cowboys.

Colt (left) with his brother Chance in June 1994—before football became priority.

The McCoy brothers—Chance, Case, and Colt (left to right)—playing in hay bales at the family ranch, Thanksgiving Day, 1995. Colt was nine years old.

Brad and Colt McCoy display the twelve-year-old's first buck, shot on the family ranch.

Coach Brad McCoy and his boys on picture day before Colt's junior, Chance's freshman, and Case's sixth-grade years. Case is following in Colt's steps as a quarterback for the University of Texas.

Colt's eighth-grade football photo, wearing the uniform of the Jim Ned Indians.

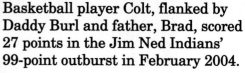

Basketball player Colt, flanked by Daddy Burl and father, Brad, scored 27 points in the Jim Ned Indians' 99-point outburst in February 2004.

Colt and GranJan, Brad's mom, share a moment after a basketball win in Colt's junior year.

At his 2005 high school graduation, Colt, wearing the insignia of the National Honor Society, poses with his father, Brad.

Colt McCoy greets Texas fans after leading the Longhorns to a 51–20 win over Kansas on November 21, 2009. The victory earned him an NCAA Division I record for most wins by a starting quarterback (43).

AP Photo/Erich Schlegel

Colt shared the basics of American football—and the message of God's love—during two mission trips to Peru with T Bar M Camps. Here, he plays catch with boys in the village of Rumococha in March 2009.

Colt McCoy celebrates a rushing touchdown in the Longhorns' 24–21 victory over Ohio State in the January 5, 2009 Fiesta Bowl in Glendale, Arizona.

AP Photo/Ross D. Franklin

The McCoy boys and mom, Debra, share a quick lunch at a hot dog stand in New York City during Colt's first Heisman trip in 2008.

Colt McCoy led the Cleveland Browns to a surprising 34–14 win over the New England Patriots in his third NFL start—a week after engineering an equally surprising 30–17 victory over the New Orleans Saints. Here, the Patriots' Josh Barrett draws a bead on the rookie quarterback.

AP Photo/Amy Sancetta

The women in Colt McCoy's life—mom, Debra, and wife, Rachel—
at Darrel K Royal–Texas Memorial Stadium before the Longhorns' game
against Baylor in 2008. Colt and Rachel were married in the summer of
2010.

Colt

I can still feel the sting of losing the state championship, but my dad helped me see that this would be a great learning experience, one I could grow and mature from.

One season had ended, and another one was about to begin—the college football recruiting season.

Little did I know that *that* season would play out long before the start of my senior year of high school.

CHAPTER 8

RECRUITING SEASON

Colt

Because of our playoff run to the 2003 Texas 2A state championship football game, I joined the Jim Ned basketball team a month late.

Shortly after Christmas break, Coach Mike Tolleson from the University of Texas showed up in Tuscola to watch me play hoops. This time he brought somebody along—Coach Greg Davis. I knew my Texas football, and I knew Coach Davis was the Longhorns' offensive coordinator *and* a decision-maker on whether to offer me a scholarship.

My stock had gone up, especially after I had set all kinds of passing records on the way to being named first-team all-state for Texas 2A schools. Dad had a lot of highlights to choose from while updating my recruiting tape. I also think Dad's cover letter pointing out the nice round number of fifty touchdowns in one season prompted coaches to pop in the tape and take a look.

Many of those coaches called Dad after the season was over to express an interest in having me come to their college or university to play football. He heard from Notre Dame, Michigan, Michigan State, Penn State, and most of the Big 12 Conference schools. Because of my high academic scores, Ivy League schools like Harvard, Yale, and Columbia also expressed interest, as did Duke of the Atlantic Coast Conference and Stanford of the Pac-10. In-state, all the big football schools inquired about me, from Texas A&M to Texas Tech to TCU to the University of Houston.

Then the University of Texas Longhorns showed their hand by sending Coach Tolleson and Coach Davis to Tuscola to watch me play basketball. I learned later on that they were there to evaluate my leadership on the basketball floor. They told my dad they noticed how driven I was to play well, run the offense from my point guard position, and hustle on defense.

Brad

Coach Tolleson and Coach Davis asked around about Colt and talked to my assistant coaches as well as Jim Ned teachers and administrative staff. They learned about his straight-A report cards and how he picked up trash by the side of the road as part of the Don't Mess with Texas program. They listened as people told them about how he worked with Meals on Wheels to deliver meals to shut-ins and how a couple of times a week he tutored elementary school kids in reading as part of Jim Ned's Peer Assistance Leadership class. They were delighted to hear that Colt supported the kids who played other sports at Jim Ned—like baseball, softball, and tennis—by coming to their games and cheering them on.

These things demonstrated what coaches call the "intangibles" about an athlete—the parts of his character that don't show up on the stat sheet. College football recruiters have learned that when it comes to the type of athlete they want to recruit, character really does count. And Colt demonstrated the kind of character they valued in their players.

Colt

Coaches try to learn as much as they can about the athlete before they offer him a scholarship. That's because they only have fifteen to twenty full-ride scholarships (meaning scholarships that pay for tuition, books, and room and board) available each year.

The first day a college football recruit can officially accept a scholarship offer is called National Signing Day, which is on the first

Wednesday in February. Once the player signs on the dotted line, there's no turning back. (There are rare exceptions to that rule, such as when there's a coaching change. But by and large, once a player signs what is called a "letter of intent," he's committed to the school and the school is committed to him.)

Only high school seniors can officially bind themselves to a school on National Signing Day. After that day passes, the new recruiting season starts, and next year's high school senior class becomes the focus of a school's recruiting efforts. After National Signing Day, most of the top college football programs immediately start recruiting the "blue-chippers"—the elite athletes who outclass their competition—and offer them scholarships in the spring of their junior year, five months or so before the start of their final season of high school football.

Even though the college can offer a scholarship in writing before National Signing Day, the recruit can only make a verbal acceptance—which is non-binding—of that offer. That said, it's expected that your "yes" be a "yes" when it comes time to officially sign that letter of intent the following February on National Signing Day—although there are plenty of occasions when recruits change their minds at the last minute and sign with another school.

I was hoping to be one of those juniors offered a scholarship before my senior year. Sure, the University of Texas was showing official interest, but I was also being courted by all the Big 12 Conference colleges outside of Texas—schools like Oklahoma, Missouri, Kansas, and Iowa State. Louisiana State University, one of the premier programs in the country, was also recruiting me.

Texas is really where I wanted to go, so I was willing to put all those schools on hold until I heard something concrete from Coach Tolleson and Coach Davis. The Longhorn coaches, however, were playing their cards close to the vest because they had two other highly touted quarterbacks on their recruiting board: Ryan Perrilloux of East St. John High School in Reserve, Louisiana, and Mark Sanchez of Mission Viejo High School in Mission Viejo, California.

When Coach Davis checked in with us, he talked openly about where I stood with Texas—and about how the Longhorns were also recruiting Perrilloux and Sanchez. "We're planning on offering scholarships to all three of you guys, but you'll be the first because you're in-state," he said. "We think that highly of you."

While that was nice to hear, Texas still hadn't put a formal scholarship offer on the table.

Then things started happening quickly. In early May of my junior year, I received my first full-ride offer—in writing. The offer came from Texas A&M. I knew A&M would be a great school for me to attend, and I was excited to receive the Aggies' offer. But they were not the Longhorns.

When one school offers a player a scholarship, though, it seems like an instant message zips through the college football recruiting network. Once Texas A&M made its offer, it seemed like everyone else wanted to dive in. In a span of just a few days, we received about two dozen more scholarship offers. Meanwhile we kept playing a waiting game with Texas—until we received a dramatic phone call from Coach Davis: *Mack Brown wants you, and your scholarship offer to attend the University of Texas is in the mail.*

You should have seen the high-fives and hugs in our household! But even though I wanted more than anything to go to the University of Texas, I didn't accept the offer right away. I wanted to think it through, just to be sure. My parents also thought that was a wise thing to do. Louisiana State University, another great school in which to study and play football, was also doing some serious wooing—and I was listening.

But Texas had the inside track.

Then we found out that the UIL (University Interscholastic League) State Track and Field Meet was being held that May at the University of Texas campus. I was planning on going to Austin to watch several of my friends compete, so we set up a meeting with Coach Brown and Coach Davis. I wanted to gather more information and see just how badly Texas wanted me.

My entire family traveled to Austin that day: Mom, Dad, my brothers, and myself. After we arrived at the UT campus, we made our way to Darrell K Royal Stadium, where the Longhorns play, and took an elevator to Coach Brown's office. One thing I'll never forget about that elevator ride is the music—"The Eyes of Texas" was playing in the background.

When we walked into Mack Brown's impressive office, the famous Texas coach welcomed us like long-lost family members and then introduced us to his wife, Sally, and to Coach Greg Davis and his wife, Patsy. Then he asked us to sit down on couches covered in burnt orange leather.

Coach Brown's office had plate-glass windows that overlooked the stadium. "Great view, isn't it? Most people don't get the chance to come and look outside and see where they have to produce every day, but this is something I get to do," he said with his country voice.

Case, in the sixth grade at the time, went over and looked at the leather saddle in Coach Brown's office and at a glass box containing all the championship rings. I couldn't believe it when my youngest brother walked over and showed me his hands. On each finger he wore a huge championship ring.

Brad

It was a relaxed, family-like atmosphere. By this point in the recruiting process, Colt and I had sat through tons of meetings in college football coaches' offices, so we were accustomed to this sort of setting—as well as the pressures coaches can apply on kids to get them to attend their school.

I had heard that Coach Brown was the best recruiter in the business and that nobody was better at closing the deal. When he gets a kid—and the parents—in the room and starts talking about what he and the school can do for them . . . well, as the old saying goes, Coach Brown could sell ice to the Eskimos. He's fantastic at what he does.

When Coach Brown started his pitch, I knew there was no way Colt would walk out of the office without saying yes to Texas.

Colt

Dad was right. Coach Brown can be very persuasive when he gets on a roll. As he was catching his breath one moment, I held up my hand: "I've heard enough, Coach. This is where I want to play—at the University of Texas. I'm going to be a Longhorn."

The room exploded into cheers. Coach Brown jumped out of the couch and hugged me and then Mom and Dad. It was a yee-hah moment of celebration.

After the commotion died down and we returned to our seats, Coach Brown had one more thing to say.

"Okay, this is how it works," he began. "I just offered you a scholarship. I got down on my knee, asked you to marry me, and you said yes. So we put the ring on the finger, and now we're engaged. You can't go anywhere else because if you do, then you're breaking our engagement. So you're coming to Texas. That's it. Tell everybody. Tell all the coaches, 'Thanks, but no thanks, I'm going to Texas, and I'm going to go play for Mack Brown.' And that's how it works."

I appreciated the down-home explanation. I was betrothed to the University of Texas, and I couldn't have been any happier.

Coach Brown didn't have to worry about me entertaining other suitors. I didn't visit any other schools, and I didn't contemplate any more recruiting visits—even though scholarship offers continued to pour in.

Meanwhile, coaches and scouts continued to make the trek to Tuscola. Stanford University's coaching staff had seen some video of me, and one of their coaches flew from California to Abilene, then jumped into a rental car and drove down to Jim Ned—with a scholarship offer in hand. The Stanford coach reported to the front desk and asked to see my dad. Nobody knew he was coming.

When the coach stepped into my father's office, he got down to business. "We've never seen your son in person," he said. "We've watched him on film. We want to offer him a scholarship. We've heard all this great stuff about him."

"Well, he just verbally committed to Texas," said my father. "Sorry, but you're too late."

There was no more to say. Five minutes later, the coach was back in his rental car and drove back to Abilene to catch the return flight to California.

Mom and Dad were happy and really excited that I had verbally committed to Texas. Now that decision wouldn't be hanging over my head throughout my senior year of football. Also, since I was an in-state player, they would be able to attend all my home games and some road games as well. We didn't talk about this, but since money was always tight in our household, I'm sure they were relieved that they wouldn't have to pay for my college education.

∾

I still had one more season of high school football to play, and as far as I was concerned, there was some unfinished business. We had a great core of guys coming back that year, and we all figured we had enough gas in the tank to make another run for the state championship.

The highlight of my senior year was playing with my brother Chance, who was a sophomore. Chance had played quarterback on the junior high and junior varsity teams, but this year there was a senior quarterback at Jim Ned in his way.

Chance didn't want to sit on the bench all season, so before training camp that summer, he approached the head coach and asked, "Dad, why don't you let me play receiver?"

Actually, we needed another receiver. We ran a spread offense a lot of the time, which meant I lined up five yards behind center—called the "shotgun" formation—and directed an offense that was "spread" across the line of scrimmage. We used multiple wide receivers in that formation, usually four.

Chance wanted to be that guy we needed. He wasn't extremely fast, but he was fast enough and quick enough to play receiver. He was close to my height and had a large pair of hands, which, we found out in practice, were good at catching the ball. Dad installed Chance at one of our wide receiver positions, and he and I had an awesome year. He caught everything I threw in his direction and made plays. He really stepped up, which was impressive since he had to learn a new position after playing three seasons at quarterback.

Chance was the second-born son in our family, and like most brothers two years apart, we played and fought and argued and laughed together as we grew up. But having the chance to play with Chance—I love saying that—turned out to be a sweet experience. I loved having my brother as one of my main targets, and with Dad coaching us to win after win—well, football just couldn't get any better.

Playing with Chance on Friday nights deepened our relationship.

He wasn't driving yet, but I was, so he and I drove everywhere together, which meant he started hanging out with my friends. Not only did Chance and I develop a closer relationship, but dinner table conversations with Mom and Dad were a lot of fun that season. Why not? We were winning every game, I was throwing passes, and Chance was catching them. What was there not to like?

Another thing I liked about my senior year was that Chance caught my first touchdown pass of the season and that my last touchdown pass of my high school career also landed in his arms. Those "bookend" touchdowns felt pretty cool, and for the season, Chance caught fourteen TD passes, or one a game.

With Chance reinventing himself as a wide receiver, some may wonder why I didn't throw to my brother every time. For one thing, defenses would have adjusted. Besides, I had three other very good receivers at my disposal, including senior Cameron Holson, who stood 6 feet, 5 inches tall and was my best friend.

Remember how Dad said there were a lot of talented sixth graders in Tuscola when we were looking at going there nearly six years earlier? Cam was one of those gifted athletes. He was an all-state receiver with glue-like hands and my leading receiver throughout my high school career. Cam was the guy I looked for when we needed a big play.

We became very close friends during high school, and later we were in each other's weddings. After graduating from Abilene Christian, where he played basketball, Cam returned to Tuscola, where he's now working for an ecological survey group.

Another interesting thing happened midway through our season: one Saturday morning, I received a phone call from Coach Brown.

Wait a minute. Texas was getting ready to play Oklahoma in the Red River Rivalry game at the Cotton Bowl in Dallas. Kickoff was just a few hours away.

"Colt, how ya doin'?" Coach Brown said, sounding like he didn't have a care in the world. "I just want you to know that you're going to be here in Dallas with us next year. You're going to play against Oklahoma someday."

I thanked Coach for taking a couple of minutes to call me in the midst of his team's pregame preparations. You better believe I watched the game on TV, but Texas lost 12–0—their only loss in 2004.

Brad

Like Texas, Jim Ned High had another banner year. We went through our regular season undefeated, setting us up for another run at the state championship. We lost 37–27 in the semifinals to Canadian High, the eventual state champions, but this time there were no tears. Colt and his teammates had played their hearts out, and they had nothing to be ashamed about.

Just like that, Colt's high school football career was in the books. He won 26 of 28 games he played his junior and senior years, took us deep into the state championship playoffs two of his three seasons, was twice named all-state (first team) by the Texas Sports Writers Association—along with Offensive Player of the Year two times—and threw for 9,344 yards—more than *five miles* of passing yardage. His 116 touchdown passes meant he averaged nearly three TDs per game. Nobody in Texas 2A football history had ever passed better or for more yards.

Colt

Besides the postseason awards, I received something else once the season was over: my first truck. (Daddy Burl let me use his old beat-up farm truck after I turned sixteen, but that doesn't count.)

Actually, the truck was a result of my parents fulfilling a commitment they had made to me six years earlier when I was in sixth grade. I had been hanging around the locker room at Hamlin, and I listened in as the high school football players talked about what cars and trucks and four-wheelers they liked. I loved hearing them talk because I was getting to the stage where I liked cars and trucks.

"What am I going to drive when I'm in high school?" I asked my dad at dinner one night.

"That's a ways off, but I'll tell you what: if you earn a scholarship and go play football somewhere, then your mom and I will buy you a vehicle."

Dad saw me pondering this and told me I should write it down.

After dinner, I took a piece of notebook paper and wrote: *Mom and Dad promise to buy me a truck if I get a football scholarship to college.* Then I signed the piece of paper and had my parents sign it, too.

I never forgot doing that, and now that I would be formally accepting the University of Texas' full-ride scholarship offer the first week of February, I reminded my parents of their pledge.

"Good for you. You remembered," my dad said. "What kind of car were you thinking of?"

"Actually, I was thinking of a truck, and I'd love it to be a 4x4. Otherwise, I don't care what kind of truck you get."

Nothing like asking for what you want.

After basketball practice a couple of days later, we went to Daddy Burl and GranJan's for dinner, and when we arrived, there was a beige 2003 Ford F-150 4x4 pickup truck parked in my grandparents' driveway. The truck had leather seats and a cool grill guard on the front—but no gun racks. The vehicle wasn't new—it was a year or so old with 25,000 miles on the odometer—but my first real truck looked fine to me.

I drove my Ford F-150 all through my years at the University of Texas, and I still drive that truck today—even though it's got 150,000 miles and I have enough money in the bank to buy a new truck. As long as my truck continues to run well, I'll keep driving it.

On January 1, 2005, I watched Texas beat Michigan 38–37 in the Rose Bowl, the bowl game nicknamed "The Granddaddy of Them All" because it's the oldest. This was the first time Texas had ever played in the Rose Bowl—or faced the Michigan Wolverines in football. It was one of those seesaw games. We'd score to take the lead, and then they'd score to take it back—it went back and forth like that until a Texas field goal late in the fourth quarter won the game for the Longhorns. Texas finished 11–1 and was ranked in the top five in the country. I couldn't wait to get to Austin.

About a week after the Longhorns played in Pasadena, just weeks before National Signing Day, Coach Mack Brown drove to Tuscola to visit.

No celebrity of that caliber had ever come to tiny Tuscola before. There wouldn't have been more hoopla if President George W. Bush himself had come into town in a long motorcade of black Suburbans with tinted windows.

Coach Brown drove straight to Jim Ned High School, and for the next two hours, he signed autographs and had his picture taken with the starstruck students. He met all my teachers and the rest of my family.

A large group of us invited Coach Brown to have lunch at Perini Ranch Steakhouse in Buffalo Gap, where the mesquite-smoked rib eye steaks are to die for. My dad, my other high school coaches, and some school administrators sat around and listened as Coach Brown told stories about the glory days at Texas.

After lunch Coach Brown visited Mom's elementary school

and talked to the kids in her PE class. There wasn't a hand he didn't shake or a hug he didn't accept.

I thought it was really nice of Coach Brown to come to Tuscola, but it wasn't necessary at all. I wouldn't be having any eleventh-hour change of heart.

On the morning of February 2, 2005, I sat at a table set up for me in the Jim Ned school library. With my teammates, friends, and teachers looking on, I took a deep breath and signed my name to the University of Texas' tendered offer.

I was going to be a Longhorn, and I couldn't have been happier.

Then the news got better. Remember how Texas wanted to sign another quarterback—either Ryan Perrilloux from southern Louisiana or Mark Sanchez from Southern California?

Mark Sanchez, to the surprise of no one, chose Pete Carroll's top-notch program at the University of Southern California. That was okay with Texas fans, though, because Ryan Perrilloux had given Coach Brown a verbal commitment back in August, just before the start of his senior year. (I'm sure Coach gave him the same "we're engaged" speech that he gave me.)

Six months later, on National Signing Day, Ryan changed his mind and eloped with LSU. I guess there was a lot of pressure on him to stay close to home.

One less quarterback that I have to beat out, I thought.

Once the news of Perrilloux's change of heart got out, the focus was suddenly on me.

Who's this kid from Tuscola? What does Mack Brown see in him? the fans and the media wondered.

Reporters who covered the Longhorns for the state's major newspapers openly questioned why Coach Brown had offered me a scholarship in the first place. Everybody knew Texas quarterbacks came from powerhouse high schools in major metropolitan areas, not backwater schools in flyspeck towns that weren't big enough to have a stoplight.

He's a 2A guy. He's a clipboard holder. He's never going to make it.

That was okay with me, though. As far as I was concerned, it was more fuel for the fire.

Eventually, things calmed down, and college football would start soon enough. We had fun the last couple of months of high school, like the time when we were ahead of the lesson plan in our College Prep class. On one Friday afternoon, the teacher let us play foursquare.

Yes, I'm talking about the playground game for first graders where four individuals each take their positions in a square quadrant and pass around a ball and try to keep it from hitting the floor. Even our foursquare games brought out my competitive nature, and my teacher nearly had a heart attack when I dove for the ball and hit the deck, trying to save myself from losing.

"Colt, what would Mack Brown say?" the teacher asked.

But the story that probably epitomizes those last few carefree days of high school took place in my geography class. Coach Williamson, Dad's offensive coordinator, taught that class, and he liked to add a bonus question to his tests and quizzes—usually riddles or brain twisters that forced you to think. I usually didn't get many right, but then again, neither did anyone else in my class.

But one time I was just sure I knew the answer to this question:

Mary's mother has five daughters. They are Nana, Nene, Nini, Nono, and _ _ _ _.

This four-letter name was easy. There are five vowels, right? A-E-I-O-U . . . which meant the fifth *had* to be *Nunu*.

I finished my test, proud of myself for having solved the riddle. I walked toward Coach Williamson and slapped my test on his desk.

"Gotcha this time, Willy!" I announced for all to hear.

"Good for you, Colt. We'll see if that's true when everyone hands in their test," he replied.

After collecting all the exams, Coach Williamson found mine and looked at the bonus question. "All right, Colt," he said in front of everyone. "You finally got one right. Tell us how you came up with the answer."

I marched up and stood before the class. "Well, if you look at the progression of vowels, the last one has to be *Nunu*."

"But what about Mary?" asked Coach.

"Mary?" And then my heart sunk . . . . *Mary's mother has five daughters* . . . .

The class laughed uproariously, and my face turned as red as our Indian team jerseys.

To this day, whenever I run into Coach Williamson, he still calls me *Nunu*.

CHAPTER 9

UT, HERE I COME

Colt

I couldn't wait to start college, so it was a good thing I didn't have to wait very long.

One week after I walked with my class into the Jim Ned gymnasium with the school band's rendition of "Pomp and Circumstance" playing, I found myself loading boxes of clothes, my CD collection, and various other stuff into the bed of my pickup truck. I was packing up because I was starting college at the University of Texas the following Monday.

The University of Texas coaches strongly recommended that all incoming freshmen enroll in summer school to start strength and conditioning training as well as attend a couple of introductory classes to ease their way into college life. There were two one-month semesters of summer school, one in June and one in July. One of the obligatory classes for incoming freshmen was a College 101–type class that would teach me how to study, make friends on campus, and figure out my way around the University of Texas, which was a small city in itself. The undergrad and graduate enrollment at UT was fifty thousand students.

Back in Tuscola, Mom and Dad gave me a hand packing up my truck, and then we put more of my stuff in their pickup—because they were coming along to help me get settled into my dorm room and see me off on this grand adventure. I was the oldest child leaving home for college, so Mom was feeling a bit emotional. It was the first weekend of June, and she didn't have much time to mentally prepare herself for her first child leaving

145

the nest so soon after high school graduation.

At first Mom rode with me while Dad followed in his truck, and when we got closer to Austin, she and Dad switched for the last part of the three-and-a-half-hour journey.

It wasn't hard to see where we were going—Jester Residence Center, a cluster of reddish-beige high-rises dominated by fourteen-story Jester West and ten-story Jester East. I would be living in Jester East, where the athletes were housed on the third and fifth floors. We had an athletic dining hall that was open to all students, but meals were free for athletes on scholarship.

It was a madhouse as I checked in and moved into my room, which came with a twin bed and a desk. I would be sharing a bathroom with the room next door, where Jermichael Finley, who was coming in as a tight end, would live as my suitemate. (Jermichael now plays for the Green Bay Packers, and in 2011 he just won his first Super Bowl ring.) One of the good things about my dorm room was that I could lock the bathroom door, as well as the door leading to the hallway, so I could have some privacy.

I'll admit moving to Austin was a bit of a culture shock for me. I don't want to give the impression that I'm a country hick, a hayseed who'd never visited the big city before, but I had attended a school with seventy people in my graduating class. Now, here I was at Jester, the largest residence hall in North America when it was built in 1969, where three or four more times as many people from my senior class lived *on just my floor.* The entire Jester Residence Center occupied a full city block and housed more than three thousand students. Jester even had its own zip code.

Despite all the commotion, I knew Jester Hall would be my home for at least the next two years. That's because Coach Brown made it mandatory that all football players stay four semesters in the athletic dorms.

In the coming weeks, I learned why my floor was called "The Dirty Third." (During my second year at Texas, I would move to "The Filthy Fifth.") Some of my peers, I discovered, didn't mind living in a pigsty. Daddy Burl's horse stalls back on the ranch were cleaner than their rooms. The communal bathroom was vile, and students left cafeteria trays full of dirty dishes outside their rooms like they were living in a hotel. The smells were rank.

All those discoveries were ahead of me that first day I arrived in Austin. After getting checked in and settled, I went out to dinner with Mom and Dad, and then they kissed and hugged me good-bye before heading back home.

Brad

Getting Colt unpacked in his dorm room was an emotional time for Debra and me. But we knew the coaches were nurturing, and they assured us Colt was going to be fine.

We spent a lot of time on the drive back home praying for Colt and for the transition *we* were going through. In many ways, it felt to us like the end of an era because Debra and I would soon be moving to Graham, Texas, where I had accepted a new head coaching and athletic director position at Graham High School.

We had been very happy at Jim Ned, but I had been offered various coaching jobs over the years because my teams had been so successful. When Graham's school superintendent, Dr. Beau Rees, contacted me, we formed a bond. He was a great guy, and he kept offering me the job and sweetening the pot until I accepted.

I said yes for several reasons: First, I would be moving up another rung on the coaching ladder by serving at a bigger school—Graham was 3A. Our move also meant that Chance would see an upgrade in competition on the football field. In addition, our youngest son, Case, was entering eighth grade and, like his oldest brother, wanted to play quarterback. I was looking out for his future as well.

The move to Graham worked out very well for us. Case was a talented quarterback who would win the starting position as a freshman. So for Case's first year of varsity high school football, Chance was his primary target.

"I got a chance to make both my brothers look good," Chance quipped. But he would play so well that he earned himself a football scholarship to my old school, Abilene Christian, where I had played wide receiver. I guess the acorn doesn't fall very far from the tree.

There was another advantage in moving to Graham, even though it was about forty miles farther from Austin than Tuscola was. Living in Graham put us much closer to a major airport. Living a hundred miles west of Dallas–Fort Worth meant it would be a lot more convenient for us to take flights to watch Colt in road games—if he won the starting job at Texas in coming years.

If we could afford it, we weren't about to miss game day if Colt was playing, but nothing was sure at that time.

Colt

My grandparents and my aunt and uncle gave me a lot of support as I headed off to college, and they made a big deal out of it because I was the first grandchild or nephew to leave home and attend a university.

There was some worry on their part, which was only natural. Everybody in my family had gone to Abilene Christian University, and as the name implies, ACU was a Christian college. (ACU is affiliated with the Church of Christ.) ACU's mission statement declared that it was the school's goal to prepare students for Christian service and leadership throughout the world.

The University of Texas, on the other hand, was a public university—and proudly secular to boot. While UT is a respected academic institution that *U.S. News & World Report* had ranked thirteenth among public schools, everyone knew about the school's well-earned reputation as one of the top party schools in the country. UT had one of the biggest Greek systems in the country, and toga parties often spilled out onto the sidewalks along frat row.

I was well aware that many Christian kids fall away from their faith when they go off to college, especially one as large as UT, where it would be easy to get swallowed up by a different crowd. Daddy Burl spoke to me about that before I left for Austin. His advice to me was, *Don't ride the fence.* He painted this word picture because we used to build fences together when I was growing up, so I would understand what he was talking about.

"You can't ride the middle of the fence," Daddy Burl said. "You've got to pick a side and live with it. If you want to pick a side where there are crazy parties and you can do whatever you want and don't have to live for anything and don't have any goals and want to go through life doing your own thing, then you have to choose that side of the fence and live with it.

"Or you can get on this other side of the fence, where you know your goals, know your priorities, know your faith, know who you want to be, and know where you want to go. But you have to be *all in* on this side of the fence. You can't sit in the middle of the fence and have one foot on one side and one foot on the other because if you do that, you are lukewarm. That is what Jesus tells us not to be."

With Daddy Burl's words ringing in my ears, it took me about fifteen minutes after I arrived in Austin to realize that I was no longer under my parents' roof and that I could do pretty much what I wanted to. But I had already decided which side of the fence I would live on, so Daddy Burl and the rest of the family had nothing to worry about. I felt rock solid in my faith because of what they had taught me over the years. I knew how I wanted to live my life and what was important to me.

For me, the first part of living on this side of the fence was figuring out which people I wanted to become friends with and hang out with. I wanted to make sure I developed friends who thought like I thought and who shared my values and goals. But please don't get the idea I would hang out or become friends only with Christian guys and gals. At Texas I made friends with tons of people from all walks of life, and if you were my teammate, you automatically became my friend.

I already had one good buddy waiting for me to arrive: Jordan Shipley, the son of Dad's college roommate at Abilene Christian. Jordan and I went way back because our fathers went way back. They were close friends at ACU, where Dad played wide receiver and Bob was the running back on the football team. After Bob graduated, he married and set off to become a high school football coach, just like Dad.

The McCoys and the Shipleys kept in touch, had kids at the same time, visited each other at Daddy Burl's ranch, and vacationed together at summer church camps. Jordan was born nine months before I was, and we were inseparable whenever our families got together. We loved doing fun things like fishing, four-wheeling, and playing one-on-one basketball. We also loved playing football, and Jordan would run routes while I passed him the ball. Jordan became quite a receiver in high school, and he had also been offered a scholarship to play at the University of Texas. The prospect of throwing to one of my childhood friends at the collegiate level thrilled me.

The first weekend I was in Austin, Jordan and I attended the University Avenue Church of Christ, which was located on campus.

That helped instill a habit we maintained throughout my five years at UT. To me, going to church was one of those nonnegotiables, which GranJan was glad to hear. My grandmother called me on a few Sundays during my first semester, asking if I had been to church. Nothing like having your grandmother holding you accountable.

I looked to Jordan and several other guys to become my accountability team at UT. I knew they would hold my feet to the fire, and I would hold them accountable as well.

I didn't want to be one of those young people who walked away from his faith at college. My faith in Christ was more important to me than football, which meant that I couldn't just mail it in. I had made a commitment to stay strong in the Lord many years earlier, and nothing would change that commitment after I became a college student—despite the temptations that would come my way.

Living on the side of the fence I did is the main reason I found it easy to say no when I was asked to drink, which happened often in the early days. As I said before, I didn't drink in high school, and I certainly wasn't about to start drinking at UT—not when it was illegal, not when I was on scholarship, and not when I had a goal of one day becoming the starting Longhorn quarterback.

Even though I didn't drink, I still went to my share of parties during my five years at Texas. I loved hanging out with my friends and my teammates, sharing laughs and swapping stories. My friends all knew I had chosen not to drink, and they respected me for what I believed in. Even though my friends knew I wasn't a partier, at least when it came to drinking, we still had a great time hanging out until it was time for me to go to bed. Then I would call it a night and head back to the dorm.

I was really glad to have my own dorm room at Jester East; otherwise it would have been impossible to go to sleep at a decent hour. During my first summer on campus, I wanted to be asleep by 10:00 every night because preseason workouts for incoming freshmen started at 6:00 a.m. Woe to those who didn't arrive on time! (The returning players were scheduled to arrive for their workouts at 8:00 and 10:00 a.m.) I quickly learned why our coaches required the fresh recruits to come in at 6:00 in the morning. They laid down the idea early that if you want to play Texas football, then you'd better be ready to pay the price, even at the crack of dawn.

Our early morning Monday-to-Friday workouts were extremely grueling. People called our strength coach, Jeff Madden, "Mad Dog," and there was a good reason for it. Sometimes he went crazy on us. The players all feared him to death, especially those who had partied the night before. The new recruits usually got the message that the pain was not worth the "gain" of staying out late.

The entire Texas football team, with a couple of exceptions, had enrolled in summer school. The guy everyone kept their eyes on was quarterback Vince Young, who was coming off a breakout sophomore season in 2004, when he started every game and led the team to an exciting victory over Michigan in the Rose Bowl.

I first met Vince in the locker room, and I remember feeling intimidated because he and the other juniors and seniors looked so much older, bigger, and stronger than I did.

"I heard there was a new quarterback in town," he said, sticking out his hand. "Welcome to Texas."

"Thanks, Vince. I'm glad to be here."

"We're having a seven-on-seven starting in thirty minutes," he told me. "I want you to come join us."

NCAA rules forbid coaches from holding organized practices prior to the start of training camp, so any early summer practices had to be player-led. That afternoon I walked onto the grass surface of massive-but-empty Darrell K Royal-Texas Memorial Stadium to check things out. I saw Vince organizing some stretch lines and took my place. After that, he orchestrated the seven-on-seven competition—a mini scrimmage between the offense and the defense in T-shirts and shorts. Vince called the plays on offense, and somebody on defense called the pass coverages.

I stood off to the side, holding a ball in my hand. After about fifteen minutes, Vince glanced in my direction. "Colt, get ready," he said. "I'm going to put you in." A couple of plays later, he waved me toward the huddle and then called a passing play, taking a moment to explain the terminology to me.

It was time to show my teammates what I could do.

As the huddle broke, I clapped my hands and took my position on offense. I felt nervous as I called off the snap count, but I made some good throws. Vince had me run through several plays; then he got back in there and let me watch from the sideline.

Once Vince was convinced we had our work in for the day, he announced that practice was over. As we walked back toward the locker room, our quarterback told me, "You did fine today. We're going to win a lot of games, and you're going to learn a lot. I feel like someday you're going to be the guy here. I want to teach you everything I know so you'll be ready."

"Thanks, Vince," I said. "I appreciate that."

"It's nothing. When I got here, Major taught me," he said, referring to Major Applewhite, who had set numerous school records while playing four seasons at Texas, including career completions (611), career passing yards (8,353), passing yards in a season (3,357), and completions in a season (271).

"Major helped me, and now I'm going to do the same thing for you. And one day, you're going to do the same for the next freshman who comes in."

Vince's words blew me away that day.

Little did I know that I would break all four of those passing records set by Major Applewhite at the University of Texas.

~

At the start of training camp, Coach Greg Davis got his first good look at me without my shirt on, and then he put me on a scale: 179 pounds.

"Son, get into the weight room and talk to me later."

I had been a regular in the weight room since my Jim Ned days, but even with all the lifting I did prior to coming to Texas, as well as the 6:00 a.m. summer workouts, I wouldn't be vying for Mr. Universe anytime soon. Coach Davis said I looked like a skinned squirrel compared to big dudes who had been killing the free weights. All I could do was keep working hard and pounding those protein shakes.

At the start of my first training camp at Texas, I stood in line to receive my uniform. When I reached the front of the line, the equipment manager asked, "What number?"

"Four," I replied. That had been my number for six years at Jim Ned, and I was still a big fan of Brett Favre, who wore No. 4. To me, that was my number, my identity on the field.

"Not available. Limas Sweed took it already." Limas was a wide receiver who was two years older than me, and No. 4 became available after Roy Williams, one of the great receivers in Texas history, graduated and went into the NFL after the Detroit Lions drafted him.

I couldn't ask for my second favorite number—No. 24. It didn't seem like a Texas QB number. I liked No. 24, though, because Mom wore that number when she played high school basketball, and that was my number when I played for the Jim Ned basketball team.

Time to see what other quarterback numbers were available.

"What about 8?" Two times four equaled 8, and before I was a

Favre fan, I was a huge follower of Troy Aikman and Steve Young, great quarterbacks who wore No. 8.

The equipment manager slowly shook his head. "Not available."

"What about 11?" That was Major Applewhite's number, so maybe some of his success would rub off on me.

"You can't wear Major's number," he replied.

That's what the equipment manager said, but here's what I heard: *You're not good enough to wear Major's old number.*

"The only thing I've got for you is No. 12," said the equipment manager, who I could tell was getting exasperated with me. "Take it or leave it."

"Okay," I said. So much for choosing my own number.

I've never told anyone this before, but being handed a set of No. 12 jerseys just added more fuel to the fire burning in my belly to play quarterback for the Texas Longhorns. I was sure that if blue-chip recruit Ryan Perrilloux had come to Texas, he could have picked any number he wanted. But I was a nobody from Tuscola, and the only number I could have was No. 12.

All during training camp, I made it a point to shadow Vince everywhere—from the practice field to team meetings to the film room. What he learned, I learned. What he practiced, I practiced.

As the start of the 2005 season grew near, Coach Brown told me he would be listing me as the third-string quarterback behind Vince and senior Matt Nordgren. His intention was to not play me at all that season so that he could preserve another year of eligibility for me.

I was fine with that. As everyone knew, Vince Young was a junior, so he had two more seasons of Texas football ahead of him. Barring an injury to Vince, that meant that if I took a redshirt season, I wouldn't get a shot to play until my third year of college, or my sophomore year of eligibility. I appreciated, though, how

Coach Davis brought me along by having me quarterback the scout team against the first- and second-team defense. That gave me the opportunity to get my reps and stay sharp.

I also stayed spiritually sharp during the week by participating in Fellowship of Christian Athletes (FCA) meetings, called "Huddles," on Wednesday nights. The FCA is an evangelical Christian organization that helps athletes keep a Christian outlook on campus. Our weekly meetings included fellowship, study, and accountability.

I knew FCA well. I first became involved with the Fellowship of Christian Athletes when I was in junior high at Jim Ned. I discovered the value in forming relationships with peers who believed and lived the same way I did. The FCA, which was open to non-athletes, is a great organization that made learning about God fun.

From the moment I first arrived on the UT campus, I knew it was important to plug myself into a campus ministry where I could hear godly speakers inspiring people to read God's Word and share with us great teaching from the Bible. A speaker at the FCA meetings might talk about trusting in the Lord one night and expound on a passage of scripture, such as Jeremiah 29:11, which says, " 'For I know the plans I have for you,' declares the Lord, 'plans to prosper you and not to harm you, plans to give you hope and a future.' " This inspirational verse is one of my favorites in the Bible.

I never served on the leadership team at FCA because of the demands that playing football placed on me. But I was always at the meetings and always part of FCA. Reagan Lambert, the FCA director for Austin/Central Texas, often asked me to share my faith at FCA middle school and high school Huddles, pointing out to me that kids in this age group often have a hard time finding positive role models. He said these students will often listen to college athletes when they won't listen to parents or ministers telling them the exact same things. I understood that and embraced it, and in coming years, I spoke at as many of these Huddles as I could.

I remember Reagan telling me one time that when you're the QB at the University of Texas, you have to have something to say when they hand you a microphone. "Just remember what you needed to hear when you were in middle school or high school," he told me.

On another occasion, I asked Reagan if there was anything I could do for the annual FCA "Sharing the Victory" fund-raising banquet.

"Sure," he said. "Could you stand next to the elevator and point guests to the ballroom?"

"No problem," I said, and that's what I did—greeted guests as they stepped off the elevator and said, "Right this way, folks."

I joined another organization after I arrived in Austin: the Texas Cowboys, a service organization on the UT campus dating back to 1922. I joined so I could meet people outside of my circle of football friends—to broaden my horizons—as well as to give back to the university community. The Texas Cowboys hosted faculty receptions, capital campaign events, and various other University of Texas ceremonies, all of which I participated in.

The Texas Cowboys also manned "Smokey," the six-foot tall, half-ton cannon they fired off every time the Longhorns scored a touchdown.

I was never asked if I was available for "Smokey" duty at our home games.

～

The 2005 season was a fun one to watch from the sidelines, especially if you like winning every game. We were demolishing opponents—we beat Baylor 62–0 and later destroyed Colorado 70–3 in the Big 12 championship game—and some were saying we could be the greatest Texas team ever. But to make good on those claims, we would have to beat the No. 1–ranked University of Southern California Trojans in the 2006 BCS National Championship at the Rose Bowl in Pasadena.

It was No. 1 versus No. 2, a classic matchup of two undefeated heavyweight programs that were both 12–0.

The team trip to Los Angeles was tremendously exciting. It was my first time in Southern California, so I soaked up everything, including our visits to Disneyland and Hollywood.

After our team meeting the night before the national championship game, Vince called me over to have a word with him.

"I just wanted you to know first. I'm out. I'm done," Vince said.

"What are you saying?" I wasn't sure if I had heard right.

"After this game, I'm leaving for the NFL," he replied. "I'm turning it over to you. I taught you everything I know. I know you're going to do great. You've got a lot of work to do, but I'm fully confident you'll be ready to go."

I thanked Vince and wished him all the best, but the news stunned me. Rumors of Vince skipping his senior year to enter the NFL draft had been swirling for months. Now that Vince confirmed to me that he was leaving, the quarterback position at UT was suddenly open. Also, our second-string quarterback, Matt Nordgren, was graduating, leaving me first on the depth chart.

All this meant I had a wide-open opportunity to earn the spot the following season. I had heard that a high school All-American, two-time all-state 4A quarterback from Stephenville High School in Texas, Jevan Snead, had verbally committed to Texas, but I decided I would worry about that if and when he actually signed.

In the meantime, I would watch the BCS Championship Game from the Rose Bowl sideline with a different perspective, knowing that Vince was playing in his final collegiate game.

Every Texas fan knows what happened during the last two

minutes of the big game. We were down 38–33 late in the fourth quarter, and our defense had just stuffed the Trojans' LenDale White on a fourth-and-two, giving us the ball on our own 44-yard line.

We had life, but it would take a touchdown to win the game.

Vince drove us down the field as the clock ticked away. On a second-and-10 from the USC 13-yard line, he scrambled for five yards and then called time-out. The Rose Bowl fans were going crazy, and both sides knew the game was building to a storybook climax.

Vince jogged toward the sideline, helmet pushed halfway up his head, to talk with Coach Brown. Clipboard in hand, I leaned into the huddle to hear the play call.

Vince smiled and laughed, then took a swig of water and listened to Coach Brown deliver his instructions.

He looked over and winked at me. "Take notes," he said. "You'll be here someday. This is how you do it."

"Go get it!" I yelled over the roar of the crowd.

That was typical Vince: he said he was going to do something, and then he went out and did it. After an incomplete pass to Limas Sweed, Vince stood in the shotgun on a fourth-and-five from the USC 8-yard line with 26 seconds to go. He took the snap, scanned the field for his receivers, and when he couldn't find anyone open, he took off on a diagonal for the right pylon of the end zone. He won the footrace, and Texas won the national championship.

My teammates and I all jumped for joy, but I can't say I was really surprised. Before Vince's dash for the end zone, I already believed he would get it done, just as he had said he would.

That night I dreamed about what it would be like to be in the same position someday—the BCS National Championship, fourth-and-goal, down by four, and precious seconds ticking away.

I wanted a chance to make a play fans would talk about for a long time.

CHAPTER 10

THE EYES OF TEXAS ARE UPON ME

Colt

When I signed my letter of intent at Tuscola High School on National Signing Day in early 2005, I was the only quarterback among the fifteen players who signed with the Longhorns.

College football gurus later downgraded UT's 2005 recruiting class to No. 20, no doubt because Ryan Perrilloux had stayed in Louisiana *and* because they didn't believe my quarterbacking skills were good enough for a high-powered program like Texas. Then Vince Young had his monster season, prompting him to head for the greener pastures of the NFL. Longhorn fans were left wondering: *Who will Mack Brown bring in to replace one of the great quarterbacks in Texas history?*

This all explains why there was such a flurry of excitement among Texas fans when Jevan Snead, the highly touted quarterback from Stephenville High, announced he was coming to Texas after backing out of a verbal commitment to the University of Florida. He changed his mind after the Gators landed a recruit named Tim Tebow.

In fact, Jevan doubled down by enrolling at the University of Texas right after National Signing Day so he could make himself eligible for spring football practice in April and get a head start on learning the Texas way of doing things. That made Jevan a "greenshirt" on our football team and my main competition for leading the Longhorn offense.

Those same gurus who had downgraded my recruiting class a

year earlier ranked Texas' 2006 class as the third-best in the country, no doubt because of the presence of Jevan. Another highly regarded quarterback prospect, Sherrod Harris from Bowie High School in Arlington, had signed with the class as well.

As they say, *Game on.*

Nothing was decided after three weeks of spring football, so all I could do was keep working harder, watch film longer, and work out after practice was over. I ate right, slept well, made good grades, and made sure I was involved with my teammates. One day my teammates cheered me on as I bench-pressed more than 300 pounds for the first time. I also had several teammates pull me aside to encourage me.

You can do it, man.

It's your time, Colt.

It's your team now.

Coach Brown and his staff made it known they wouldn't make any quick decisions on who would become the starting quarterback. They wanted the process to play itself out. A lot of people thought Jevan, or maybe even Sherrod, would be the next guy, but I was determined to fight, to compete, and to do everything my dad and the rest of my family had taught me all my life in order to win the quarterbacking job.

I prayed a lot during this time. I didn't selfishly pray that I would become the next Texas quarterback but asked the Lord to put me where He wanted me. I had a feeling that things would be awesome if things worked out the way I wanted them to—meaning I was named UT's next quarterback. But if that didn't happen, I would know God hadn't called me to be the quarterback at Texas.

A few weeks after the end of spring practice, I drove to my parents' new home in Graham for Memorial Day weekend. Mom and Dad had purchased a home on Timber Ridge Lake, a reservoir about a mile and a half long and probably 300 yards across, set in a canyon. Homes around the lake were built on land overlooking the water, which was about 100 feet below at the bottom of a steep embankment.

That Saturday, I went bass fishing with my father at Newcastle Lake, not far from Graham. We had a little competition for biggest catch of the day, which I won with a seven-pounder. Dad caught more fish though.

After we were done fishing, I headed off to Dad's high school gym for a long, hard workout. I came home around dusk, just as Momhad arrived from the supermarket, so I gave her a hand carrying bags of groceries into the house. She had bought steaks and vegetables for dinner.

Then I heard some high-pitched screaming. At first I thought some kids next door were having a birthday party, but then I heard the cries again. It sounded like a lady in distress.

"Help!" came the faint but desperate voice from across the lake. "My husband is having a seizure. Help! Call 911!"

"Tell Dad I'm going to help her," I said to Mom. "Call 911!"

I hustled as fast as I dared down the embankment to the water's edge. I was dressed in my post-workout clothes—T-shirt, shorts, and Nike flip-flops. The woman's cries for help were becoming more intense. I didn't know who was calling out across the lake, but the anguish in her voice made it sound like her husband was in deep trouble.

Dad was right behind me. When we reached the water's edge, Dad spotted an aluminum jon boat—a low-rise boat used for fishing—that belonged to our neighbors. "Let's take it with us," he said. "We may need it when we get to the other side."

Then my father noticed something. "There's no paddle," he said. "We're going to have to push the boat."

I tore off my T-shirt, shook off my flip-flops, and waded into the cold water. This was the end of May, and the water hadn't warmed up yet. I'd say it was in the mid-sixties, if that.

Dad untied the boat and pushed it toward me, and then he waded in. We started swimming in the direction of the woman's screams, bringing the boat along with us.

"This is Patina. Ken and I are on the dock. He's having a seizure. Call 911!"

I tugged on a line attached to the front of the boat while Dad pushed from the back. I churned my arms and kicked as hard as I could as we crossed the lake. Dusk had turned to darkness in a hurry, and there was no moon in the sky. We couldn't see anything around us except for a few lights from homes above the lake. All we could do in the pitch darkness was keep swimming toward the woman's cries of distress.

Brad

I told Colt to keep communicating with me because if he stopped talking, I would know that something was wrong with him. The last thing I wanted was for one of us to drown trying to save someone else's life. Pushing the little boat across the lake made it even harder to head in the direction of the screams, but I thought we might need it to get someone in distress out of the water. Also, if Colt or I got into trouble, the boat could save us from drowning.

The lake was 300 yards or so wide, about the length of three football fields. I don't know how long we were in the water—maybe five or ten minutes—before we spotted a crying woman kneeling on the dock next to her husband. He was thrashing around wildly, and she tried desperately to keep him from falling into the water. The dock was very small, no bigger than a compact car. The situation didn't look good at all.

Colt

Once I saw the dock, I took off and swam on. I hadn't swam that much since Dad was in charge of the municipal pool in San Saba, and my arms were very tired with the last few strokes.

As I hauled myself onto the wooden dock, I could see the man was in the throes of a violent seizure. He was about to pitch himself into the murky water. His wife had her hands full just keeping him from falling off the dock.

"You have to save my husband!" she cried frantically. "He can't fall into the water! He'll drown if he does!" I thought she might freak out at any moment.

"Hang on, ma'am," I said, then fell to my knees and used all my strength to move the man's convulsing body away from the dock's edge.

The man's head shook violently, and blood dripped from the corner of his lips. There was blood all over the front of his clothes. His limbs moved uncontrollably, and his head rocked back and forth.

I thought about sticking my hand into the man's mouth and pulling his tongue free, but then I remembered what happened when one of my teammates had a seizure during a basketball game at Jim Ned. My coach, Hunter Cooley, nearly had his finger bitten off when he stuck his hand into the boy's mouth to clear his air passageway. I think God protected me by giving me that memory.

Dad hauled himself onto the dock as I held the man in a strong grasp. Meanwhile, the woman, who had a flashlight with her, continued to fret. "If the EMTs don't get here soon—"

Then we heard a siren in the distance. We lived in a rural area, so the emergency medical technicians had a good seven or eight miles to travel before they reached us.

"They'll never find us. Go up to the road and tell them where we are," Dad directed. "Here, take my shoes." Back at the other side of the lake, Dad had jumped into the water with his sneakers on.

We both knew I'd probably have to make a 100-foot climb over boulders and rocks, and it was pitch black outside. I slipped on Dad's wet sneakers and raced to Timber Ridge Road so that I could flag down the EMTs. The distance from the dock to the street was several hundred yards, and a lot of that was rocky embankment.

When I reached the top of the embankment, I ran out to the street and waited for the EMT van to arrive. A fire truck and an ambulance pulled in together.

One of the firemen jumped out. "What's happening?" he asked.

"An older gentleman is having a seizure on the dock. It's pretty bad. Lots of blood."

"Can you show us the way?"

"Sure."

I led the emergency personnel, who were carrying medical supplies and a gurney, down the boulder-strewn path. After we reached the dock, they gave the man several shots to stop the seizures and hooked him up to an IV. Once the firemen had him stabilized, they strapped him to the gurney, and then my dad and I helped them carry him up and over the boulders to the ambulance. Within seconds, the ambulance—with red lights aglow and siren blaring—set off into the black night.

By this time, neighbors had gathered on Timber Ridge Road, and it wasn't long before Mom drove up in the family Suburban. On our way back home, we told her everything that had happened.

Brad

When we got back to the house, Colt and I both needed a hot shower to warm up. After our showers, I grilled some steaks, and we enjoyed a different kind of Memorial Weekend dinner. We were concerned for the man's health, and we were appreciative when a neighbor called to inform us that the older man had suffered what is called a grand mal seizure but that he was stabilized and would make it.

That's when we learned the identity of the couple on the dock. The man who had suffered the seizure was Ken Herrington, and he had suffered numerous seizures over the years and had undergone several brain surgeries. His wife's name was Patina.

Colt

I was glad to hear the good news and was thankful we had a chance to help out, but I didn't really think Dad and I had done that much.

A week or so after the incident, I was back in Austin. I had enrolled in summer school and was back into my routine: wake up early, work out, go to class, throw the football, eat, sleep—and start the routine all over the next day. I was intensely focused on winning that quarterback position.

Coach Brown approached me in the locker room one afternoon and asked, "Hey, did you save somebody's life?"

Somebody's life? I drew a blank.

"No. What are you talking about, Coach?"

"Did you swim across a lake and help some guy having a seizure?" he elaborated.

Now I remembered. "All I did was swim across our lake and help somebody get to the emergency room," I explained. "Why do you ask?"

"It seems that a Mrs. Herrington wrote a letter to the chancellor and the president of the university saying that you saved her husband's life. She also sent a copy of her letter to one of the local TV stations, and they want to do a story on what happened."

I didn't see what all the fuss was about, but I later learned that if my dad and I had arrived five minutes later, Mr. Herrington wouldn't have made it because his body was nearly worn out. That's why Mrs. Herrington wanted to tell everyone I had saved her husband's life.

It was very nice of Mrs. Herrington to say all those things about me and Dad, but I didn't think what we had done rose to the category of "saving someone's life." If anyone deserved credit, I thought, it was the EMTs who knew what to do to stabilize Mr. Herrington and stop the seizure.

There's a postscript to the story. I dropped by the home of Ken and Patina Herrington six months later to check up on Mr. Herrington, who thanked me profusely. That day I learned that Mr. Herrington was also a Longhorn—he had graduated from UT in 1968.

Then Mrs. Herrington handed me a present: one of my Nike flip-flops, which had washed up on shore near the Herrington's home.

We never did find the other flip-flop.

~

When I returned to Austin for the start of summer school, I tore a page out of Vince's playbook. He was the one who had organized the seven-on-seven scrimmages between the offense and defense, and now that he was gone, someone needed to fill in. As far as I was concerned, that was the quarterback's job, so I stepped up and quietly but firmly grabbed the reins of leadership.

I made sure I had the keys to the stadium . . . and the storage room for the bags of footballs. I got a list of the players and their phone numbers and called them to tell them when we'd have our seven-on-seven practices. I made sure everybody was there—took roll, if you will. If somebody didn't show up, I'd drop by his dorm room or pass by the dining hall to remind him that I'd like to see him out there. If enough guys couldn't make it to a particular practice, then I would set up another time.

Over that two-month period, I think my teammates saw my passion to play *and* my determination to lead.

One evening at the start of training camp, a group of seniors ate dinner with Coach Brown. They talked to Coach about all the behind-the-scenes work I had put into organizing the seven-on-seven practices. They told him how I had taken hold of these practices and kept everyone organized and working hard. As for my ability to throw the ball, they told Coach the arm was there. Every single one of them looked Coach in the eye and said, "We *know* who our quarterback is. It's Colt."

Sure, my teammates had seen how much effort I was putting into organizing the practices, but they also believed I had the talent to throw well, to read defenses, and yes, even take control of the huddle, which was a concern of my coaches—and myself.

Several of our linemen had beards, while I was still shaving peach fuzz off my chin. I was aware I was still a baby-faced, wide-eyed, and fairly scrawny nineteen-year-old trying to lead some gnarly dudes who looked much older.

Four out of our five returning linemen that season were fourth- or fifth-year seniors, and three—Lyle Sendlein, Kasey Studdard, and Justin Blalock—would go on to play in the NFL. These guys had all heard Vince Young call plays in the huddle, and now they had to listen to me, a small-town freshman quarterback, trying to tell them what to do. But I wasn't afraid. A few times in practice, I had to say, "Hey, get your head up. Listen to me."

The UT quarterback competition was settled during preseason training camp in team scrimmages played under real game conditions—with referees, a game clock, and every play being filmed for later review by the coaching staff. I performed well. I made good decisions, and I made poised throws. I wanted to win the job in a clear-cut fashion and not be part of the kind of "quarterback controversy" that happened at Texas a decade earlier between Major Applewhite and Chris Simms.

There was a sense of relief on the team when Coach Brown announced I had won the starting job before our home opener against North Texas. But there was something else he said to the media that caught my attention.

"Colt is going to be our starter, but Jevan is going to play some," Coach said. "We want to see what both players can do."

While I appreciated Coach's candor, all his words did was add more fuel to the fire.

I had a new goal: to be *the* quarterback at Texas—singular, not shared.

And to do that, I'd have to go out there and light it up.

~

Going into the 2006 season, the Longhorns were the reigning national champions and defending a 20-game winning streak that dated back to 2004. Even though Vince Young had landed with the NFL's Tennessee Titans and wouldn't be coming back, fan and media expectations were still sky high because we had lost only three starters on offense and three on defense. *Sports Illustrated* ranked us as the No. 3 team in its annual College Football Preview issue.

Coach Brown's announcement that I had won the starting quarterback position thrust me into the media spotlight. Anything affecting the University of Texas football team was news, and beat reporters covering the Longhorns suddenly wanted to know more about this kid from Tuscola, population 714.

Coach Brown had a longstanding rule that his players could

not speak to the media until they had played in an actual game—and I hadn't played a single down for Texas yet. Even a reporter from the local TV news station couldn't get a quote out of me for a story about me "saving" Ken Herrington's life.

But we all knew that once I took a snap, I would be thrown to the media wolves. So Coach Brown asked our longtime assistant athletic director for media relations, John Bianco, to prepare me for some of the questions I would receive.

John would become a good friend to me and my family over the next four years. He took me under his wing and mentored me on how to speak in short, declarative sentences without giving away too much information and without giving our opponents "blackboard material"—those slips of the tongue that come back to haunt you. (Example: *I guarantee we'll beat those guys like a drum.*)

John coached me on how to handle tough questions and keep my cool under the media's microscope. But even though he did a great job preparing me, nobody could have been ready for what happened the first two weeks of the 2006 season.

Our opener against North Texas University was expected to be a pop quiz before the "final exam" the following week against Ohio State, the top-ranked team in the country. But I didn't see things that way. I thought it was all about first impressions, and as they say, you only get one chance to make a first impression. I knew I had an opportunity to impress against North Texas, and I also knew I hadn't proved anything yet. I wanted to go out there and play as hard as I could and as well as I could to give our team a chance to win.

If I did that, Coach Brown would have no reason to give me the hook and give Jevan Snead a shot.

Well, I *did* light it up, which seems like an even more apt description of the game because our home opener against North Texas marked the unveiling of the first high-definition video screen in college sports and the largest high-def video screen in the world. Known as the "Godzillatron," the video screen dominated the south end zone of Memorial Stadium.

One minute into my Texas Longhorns career, my second pass found Limas Sweed on a skinny post route, which he turned into a 60-yard touchdown. Giving the "Hook 'em Horns" hand sign all the way, I sprinted down the field to hug Limas. The butterflies were gone, and from then on, it was an avalanche: I led the Longhorns into the end zone on six of my seven drives and threw for three touchdowns.

Jevan did get to play, but it was mop-up duty after the offense was ordered to take its foot off the gas because we were so far ahead. Final score: 56–7.

The way we had played in our lopsided victory had the football "experts" on ESPN hyperventilating about our upcoming game against Ohio State. It was another one of those No. 1 versus No. 2 matchups you don't see very often.

I know this will sound crazy, but at the time I was clueless as to how big the Ohio State game was or what it really meant. I was inside a protective bubble, and all I was thinking about was going out there and playing well. I didn't even know that two U.S. senators injected themselves into the game. Texas Senator Kay Bailey Hutchison and Ohio Senator Mike DeWine let the media know they had placed a friendly wager on the outcome: Blue Bell ice cream from Texas versus Senator DeWine's wife's homemade chocolate-covered peanut Buckeye candies.

Brad

Debra and I were new to this scene, too. But we got a better idea of what a big deal the Ohio State–Texas game was when we took our seats before kickoff. Memorial Stadium was packed to the rafters with 89,442 fans—the most ever to watch a football game in the state of Texas. About twenty minutes before game time, I noticed two guys edging through the crowd, looking for someone. Wearing business suits, dark sunglasses, and earpieces, they looked like FBI agents.

The two men approached Section 28, where Texas parents sit, and I heard one of them say, "Who's Brad McCoy?"

Debra looked at me. "What did you do?" she asked.

"Nothing."

I raised my hand. "I'm Brad McCoy. Can I help you?"

The man ignored my response and spoke into some type of walkie-talkie gadget. "We have him located. Row 32. Seat 4."

"Excuse me, but what did I do?" I asked.

"Oh nothing," the man in the business suit replied. "We work for CBS, and we just wanted to know where you'll be sitting."

The light came on. TV producers love those "cutaway" shots to parents or girlfriends. They train a camera on family members and wait for some type of reaction—like jubilation after a touchdown or a grimace after an interception. The cameras love faces, and since football players are hidden behind masks and padding, football broadcasts are filled with shots of anxious or jubilant family members—as well as crazy kids who paint their faces and bodies in school colors.

Let me tell you: knowing there was a camera aimed at Debra and me throughout the game—and pretty much throughout the rest of Colt's career—took some getting used to. You knew there was always that chance that you could be caught on national TV doing something stupid.

This situation had its lighter moments, though. We noticed that people around us would occasionally receive calls on their cell phones from friends telling them they had just seen them on national TV.

Colt

We lost decisively to Ohio State, 24–7. I didn't play badly, but it's hard for me to say that I played well because we lost.

There's something else I lost that day—my anonymity.

It happened so quickly. One day I was walking across the UT campus minding my business, just another one of the fifty thousand students, and the next day I had people trailing me or stopping me to say something or asking me for my autograph. It was really strange having another student ask me to sign his Econ notebook. *Why would anyone want my autograph?* I wondered. I was just a freshman. I was just trying to play football. Why was everything so crazy?

When they say, "the eyes of Texas are upon you," they aren't kidding. I felt eyes following me everywhere. It was like they were burning a hole in my back. Anytime I walked around campus, I had a feeling people were looking at me, or even *staring* at me.

My friends noticed what was happening. My family noticed what was happening. And there was nothing we could do about it.

I didn't want my friends to think I had changed or think better or worse of me. I didn't want my friends to think, 'Oh, he's gotten too big-time for me. He won't talk to me or call me.' " That was another thing I had to deal with.

The loss of my anonymity presented a lot of challenges. I came from a small town, and I wasn't used to all this attention or having people say nice things or mean things about me or suddenly wanting to be my friend. I just wanted to play football and to be left alone.

But that wasn't going to happen.

Brad

I remember saying to Colt, "Look at all the guys who have gone before you. Did you think they were big names when you were growing up? Of course you did."

And then I listed them: Vince Young and Major Applewhite and Chris Simms and James Street. "Do you understand that you're the next guy?" I asked. "Everybody is looking at you like they did at the quarterbacks I just named."

I reminded Colt to stay humble, to not be brash and blow people off. I said he'd have to be patient with the new demands put on his time and his life. "You have been blessed with this role, and with this role comes the responsibility to tend to others," I said. "I know you may not really understand it, and I know you'd really like to be by yourself more often, but there are new obligations you will have to fulfill."

Those obligations, first and foremost, were tending to the fans. At first Colt didn't understand why he had to give up an hour of his time each week to sign dozens of footballs, helmets, and jerseys for Texas alumni, various charities, and different events the school promoted. But those were some of his responsibilities, I reminded him, and to whom much is given, much will be expected.

None of us was used to all the attention, and Colt certainly wasn't used to dealing with the public, which always wanted a piece of his time. He also wasn't used to the fact that everything he said was fair game—on the Internet and everywhere else. Now that he was a public figure, he had some huge lessons to learn.

"You're living in a glass house," I said on more than one occasion, meaning that not only could people look in, but they could easily pick up a rock and toss it through your window.

Colt

After losing to Ohio State, we went on another winning streak— eight games. We won at home and on the road, from in front and from behind.

One win that stands out is my first Red River Rivalry game, which pits Texas against Oklahoma every year at a "neutral site"— the Cotton Bowl in Dallas, where half the stadium is dressed in Longhorn Burnt Orange and the other half in Sooner crimson. The name of the game comes from the Red River, which is the natural boundary between Texas and Oklahoma.

We fell behind early but came back strong to win 28–10. Then we blitzed Baylor, beat Nebraska in blowing snow in Lincoln, and came back from the dead—down 21–0—to defeat rival Texas Tech, 35–31.

Back in summer camp, Coach Brown had told me to do what he did: not read the newspapers or watch TV when the football analysts talked about Texas. I took his advice to heart, and perhaps that's one reason I was able to keep a level head during my freshman season.

But people in my universe—the UT campus and neighboring Austin—read the newspapers or went online to read about me and Texas football and *what a great quarterback this kid is and how we've never seen anyone like him come in here and play like this before and he's playing so well as a freshman that this kid has a great chance to win the Heisman Trophy and if he wins the Heisman then he would be the first freshman to ever do so which means Mack Brown is a genius for plucking this kid out of Tuscola because he's made everyone forget about Vince Young since he's the real McCoy with an arm like a Colt .45 so that makes him a real rock star.*

You know how the hype machine can rev up.

Most everyone on campus had access to Jester Hall, and there were girls who lived on the same floor as me. (Mom wasn't too happy when she heard about that.) Around 9:30 or so, I'd be bleary-eyed from fatigue—I was still waking up at 5:30 each morning— and I'd turn out the lights and try to fall asleep—despite the blaring stereos and people yelling in the halls.

Then the knocks on the door would start. Some of them were from random guys walking around the hallway wanting to talk football. Others came from females who *didn't* want to talk about football:

Colt, can we come see you?

Are you there, Colt? I want to say hello.

C'mon, Colt. Open up. We know you're in there.

Some of the comments were so blatantly sexual in nature that I can't repeat them in a family book like this.

This sometimes went on for hours and drove me crazy. As a rule, I didn't acknowledge the knocks, but if I did, it was to tell the people standing at my door that I was sleeping and to please leave me alone. Sleep came in spurts, and I often woke up cranky and fatigued.

I also woke up to notes that had been slipped underneath my door from girls giving me their names and cell numbers. Some offered me services that you can't even imagine.

I was being tempted, but I fought off the urge to give in and call one of those numbers. I crumpled those notes and tossed them into my trash can. I told myself: *Why would I want to be with any of those girls anyway? They're probably acting like this with all the guys!*

I must admit, however, that it wasn't as easy as I'm making it sound. If I have a struggle with anything, it would be my attraction to women, maybe because I've never had any problems with drinking or drugs or pornography. I'll have more to say about my relationships with the opposite sex in chapter 14, but I believe Satan placed these temptations in my path at Jester Hall.

One thing that kept me strong is that I knew dozens, if not hundreds, of people were praying for me—praying that I would be strong in the face of the temptations coming my way. People I didn't even know prayed for me, people from all the churches I grew up in, my grandparents' church in Abilene, prayer groups, and my family and friends. And I was praying, too.

I remember thinking these thoughts during my quiet time with the Lord back then: *I am here, Lord, and it's not because of me. It wasn't just hard work that got me here. Lord, you've placed me here at Texas, and I'm not going to take advantage of that by getting all the women, by getting all the fame.*

I knew that if I had let my guard down, I would have followed a path "like an ox going to the slaughter, like a deer stepping into a noose," as Proverbs 7:22 says. Proverbs 7 goes on to give this advice:

> *Now then, my sons, listen to me;*
> > *pay attention to what I say.*
> *Do not let your heart turn to her ways*
> > *or stray into her paths.*
> *Many are the victims she has brought down;*
> > *her slain are a mighty throng.*
> *Her house is a highway to the grave,*
> > *leading down to the chambers of death.*

Brad

During Colt's first season as UT's starting quarterback, Debra and I received phone calls from him at all hours—including the middle of the night. "Mom, Dad, I can't sleep. I can't do this anymore."

Something had to change because things were getting out of hand at Jester Hall—with girls and guys knocking on his door at all hours of the night. But Coach Brown had a firm rule: all members of the football team had to live in the dormitories for four semesters, so Colt was stuck.

I lobbied for a change, and at the end of Colt's redshirt freshman season, Coach Brown relented. "We're going to let you move off campus a semester early," he told Colt.

Colt moved in with two teammates, Jordan Shipley and Derek Lokey, who had rented a house in East Austin. It was a rough neighborhood, but at least Colt had some peace and quiet when he went to bed.

Colt settled in well with Jordan and Derek, but there was an incident the following season that led to another change. One night at 2:00 in the morning, a crazed man holding a gun stepped into the front yard and started screaming something about killing Colt.

"Daniel Colt McCoy, wake up and get outside. It's over. It's over!" he kept yelling over and over, which was pretty creepy because not many people knew Colt's real first name was Daniel.

Colt, Jordan, and Derek did the right thing: they called 911, and two squad cars raced to their house and arrested the man. It turned out he was pretty high on drugs. Not only that, he was really stupid, messing with three country boys who had deer rifles and shotguns in their home.

When Coach Brown heard about the incident, he told us, "Well, this isn't going to work either. We have to find another place for Colt to live."

I put on my thinking cap. What Colt needed was to find a place in a nice, safe part of Austin where he could rent a room from a widowed lady or a room above a garage—something quiet and unobtrusive.

Colt wasn't very impressed with my idea. "Dad, you are so out of touch," he said. "Nobody rents a room over a garage from some old lady. That is the stupidest thing I have ever heard. You're dreaming."

I was in town one Saturday afternoon and suggested that we drive around some neighborhoods and look at several apartments, but we couldn't find anything. Nothing looked very good to us.

We then looked around in a nice neighborhood called Tarry-town, about five minutes west of the UT campus. We crawled along in my pickup, and then I spotted a house that had a four-car garage separate from the residence with a living quarters above the garage.

"See, Colt, that is the kind of place I'm talking about," I said.

"Dad, I am telling you, this is Austin, Texas," Colt protested. "You live in a little bitty town, and you have no clue how people live in Austin. You're embarrassing me."

No sooner were the words out of his mouth when I noticed a blonde woman and a little boy sitting in the front yard of a good-looking home with a gated entrance in the back. Colt slunk deeper into his seat as I edged my truck to the curb. He actually punched me in the shoulder a few times and said, "You can't do this. You can't just stop and talk to people. Do not get out of this car!"

So I hopped out of the car and approached the woman, who looked to be in her mid-thirties. Her son, a blond-headed boy, was about seven years old.

"Hello, ma'am," I started. "Don't worry, I'm not crazy."

She nonetheless drew her son a bit closer but smiled. "Okay, how are you?" she said, "I'm glad you're not crazy."

"My name is Brad McCoy, and I saw you and your boy here, and I just wanted to stop and visit a second."

This mother still hadn't relaxed, so I looked for a way to break the ice. I looked at the boy. "What's your name, son?" I asked.

"My name is Charlie."

"Charlie, do you like the Longhorns? Are you a football fan?"

"Yeah."

"Who's your favorite player?"

"Jamaal Charles."

Not the answer I wanted. Jamaal was a star running back for the Longhorns at the time and now plays in the NFL.

"I like Jamaal, too, but do you like the quarterback?"

"Colt McCoy?" he asked.

"Yeah," I answered. "He's sitting right out there in the car."

By now, Colt looked like he was ready to slide his frame right through the floorboards.

"No way," said the mom.

"Yes, ma'am, he's right there."

Colt smiled weakly and waved.

I told her the story: how Colt had been living in a sketchy neighborhood and some drug-crazed guy with a gun came by in the middle of the night and threatened to kill him. Now, I told her, we had to find him a new place to live, and what we were really looking for was some type of garage apartment in a nice community where he could be as discreet as possible.

"I'm figuring that you know this area and might know somebody who would consider renting Colt a place to live," I said.

The women thought for a moment. "Well, we do have a place above our garage," she explained. "But we have never thought about renting it out. But I could talk to my husband and see what he thinks."

Now we had an opening.

"Colt, come on out here," I said, and introductions were made all around. She introduced herself as Tami Anderson and said her husband's name was Dick, but that he was out of town on a business trip.

After saying good-bye, we departed. But about two hours later, we got a call from Dick Anderson. He said he and his wife weren't sure about renting their garage apartment to Colt because they had two daughters under the age of twelve—Olivia and Lindsey. Even though Dick wasn't sold on having a college kid on his property, he was willing to meet with us and talk it through.

Colt and I returned to the Andersons' home, and they got their measure of Colt and heard what his needs were. That night Dick and Tami said yes to Colt moving into their garage apartment, and that's where Colt lived until he graduated and was drafted by the Cleveland Browns. The cozy place had a bedroom, a bathroom, and a living room with a kitchenette. Jordan Shipley later moved in with Colt, and they grilled a lot on an outdoor barbecue. With a gated entrance in the back of the home, the boys no longer had to deal with crazy people, or anyone else, in the middle of the night.

The McCoy and Anderson families have grown close over the years since Colt and I first introduced ourselves to Mrs. Anderson and her son, Charlie. We've vacationed together, and their children have grown close to our children. Even better, the Andersons are beautiful Christian people who were willing to share what God has blessed them with in an incredible way.

Another thing: Dick Anderson stands about 6 feet, 6 inches tall and was a great athlete, a man's man who played college football at SMU. I never really worried about Colt anymore after he moved into Dick's backyard.

Colt

Being allowed to live in the Andersons' apartment turned out to be a huge blessing for me. Three years later, after the Cleveland Browns drafted me and I had to move to Ohio, all of us wept as I packed my things for the move.

I guess Father knew best all along.

CHAPTER 11

ON A MISSION

Colt

When I first arrived in Austin, I got lost everywhere I drove. I had grown up in a place with lots of dirt roads, so navigating the downtown boulevards of Austin was a challenge those first few months of my redshirt freshman year at UT. That's why I started attending University Avenue Church of Christ; I could walk there from Jester East.

Once I moved off campus, though, Jordan Shipley and I decided to check out some of the other churches, starting with Westover Hills Church of Christ. We visited one time, liked it, and started worshipping there on Sunday mornings.

Jordan and I made it a point to attend the 9:15 or 10:45 service every Sunday morning after every home game *and* every road game, no matter how late we had gotten in the night before. Sometimes our team charter didn't touch down at Austin-Bergstrom airport until the wee hours. After a road game at Wyoming my senior year, our plane had landed in Austin at 4:00 in the morning. Five hours later, though, Jordan and I were sliding into a pew at Westover Hills.

It didn't matter to me if our team plane had landed at 9:00 Sunday morning; we still would have gone to Westover Hills because I looked forward to church, liked church, and as you'll read later in this chapter, needed church.

The Bible talks about the importance of fellowship with other believers (see Hebrews 10:24–25) and also tells us that when two or more believers are gathered in Jesus' name, He will be in their midst (Matthew 18:20).

I've always believed that God listens when you worship Him, which is why I always dragged my tired and often beat-up body to Sunday morning service. Even when I knew the rest of the day would be rough because I hadn't gotten much sleep and because I had to see my coaches on Sunday afternoon—that's when we went over game film from the day before—I still had to go to church. This was my time to connect with the Lord and other believers.

One of the things I liked about Westover Hills was that people generally left us alone. The elders must have gotten the word out not to treat Jordan or myself any differently than anyone else. *They're coming here to worship, so leave them be.* I appreciated that. If someone wanted to stop me and say hello, great. But please just treat me like any other person. Don't treat me like a hero.

I got involved in ministry at Westover Hills by teaching in the high school ministry a few times during the off-season, which was an awesome experience. I loved interacting with the kids.

On Sunday nights, I liked to go to the Austin Stone Community Church to hear Pastor Matt Carter preach. The 7:00 p.m. service was always lively, full of energy, and packed with UT students. There were usually two thousand people—almost all from the UT campus—at the Sunday night services. (My wife, Rachel, and I still like to go there when we're in town.) Matt is an unbelievable speaker and teacher, which made it easy for me to invite my teammates to church. Sometimes fifteen to twenty-five guys from the team joined me for Sunday night worship. Over my five years at UT, it became more and more important to have my teammates there with me.

Going into my sophomore season, I felt like I had really bonded with my teammates. We laughed a lot, and we teased each other a lot.

Of course, when my teammates found out my real name was

Daniel, they started calling me Daniel, even though I don't really like being called that. They were unmerciful.

"But my name is Colt," I'd protest.

"Right, Daniel!" came the answer.

So Daniel became my name around the locker room. In a way, that's almost a term of endearment because you have to know me pretty well to call me Daniel. It has gotten to the point where when I'm walking through a crowd and someone calls out, "Colt," I probably won't even look up. But if someone calls out, "Daniel," then I know it's probably someone who knows me, so I know I need to stop.

My linemen also liked playing the "Flinch Game" with me. This is game where you hit somebody, and if that person flinches, then you get "two," meaning you get to hit him twice and "wipe" him twice. (Translation: you get to hit him in the shoulder twice and then wipe your fingers twice where you hit him or on his face.) I'm not making any judgments here, but linemen seem to really go for this type of game.

Here's how the game worked: the UT linemen would sneak up on me and then make like they were going to hit me in the "man area," if you catch my drift, before pulling their punches. If I flinched, they had permission to punch my shoulder (preferably my left, since I throw with my right hand) and then "wipe" me twice, always going for my face. I'm telling you, it was a nasty game. I learned quickly not to flinch!

All the fun and games ended, though, as the team prepared for the 2007 season. We were rocked during the summer when Coach Brown suspended a half-dozen players following arrests for alleged illegal activities. Then our running backs coach, Ken Rucker, announced in August that he had been diagnosed with prostate cancer and would be taking a leave of absence to undergo surgery.

On the field, there were question marks about our offensive line. We had lost four starters to graduation, which meant we had to retool the foundation of our offense. Without a good offensive line, we couldn't run the ball and I wouldn't have as much time to throw. (It's amazing how much better I can pass when a formidable offensive line gives me an extra second.) Lastly, three of my receivers—my roommate Jordan Shipley, Limas Sweed, and Billy Pittman—were either out with injuries or playing hurt.

Even though we won our first four games and were ranked No. 7 in the polls, our offense just wasn't clicking the way we wanted it to. Our offensive line was changing every week because guys were getting hurt. Defenses have a way of finding chinks in an offense's armor, and I noticed they were taking advantage of our weaknesses.

All the shuffling of bodies resulted in inconsistency on offense, and when the offense is inconsistent, the blame is usually directed at the quarterback. I started feeling the pressure, and it only increased because I wasn't playing as well as I would have liked. I've played quarterback at the University of Texas and in the NFL, so I know that the two are very much alike. Even if you don't read the newspapers or listen to TV, you still hear some of the things being said, and you know you're getting the blame for everything that goes wrong.

Things went terribly wrong when unranked Kansas State came to Austin on September 29. The media described the game as a "tune-up" for the Red River game against Oklahoma the following week. I knew what the fans expected: that we'd handle Kansas State easily and then get ready to go to the Cotton Bowl the following Saturday to play the Sooners.

It didn't quite happen that way. I had my worst day in a Texas uniform. All day long, a relentless Wildcat pass rush pushed me out of the pocket or smothered me with sacks. I hurried too many passes or threw the ball away too many times. When I did have time to throw, the other team caught too many of my passes. The Wildcat defense ran my first interception—I had four picks that day—back 41 yards for a touchdown.

Kansas State pounded us 41–21, the worst home defeat in Coach Brown's ten years at Texas. Now the Red River game was coming up. Oklahoma was ranked higher and favored, but we thought a victory over the Sooners would turn around a season going south.

Sooners quarterback Sam Bradford was a redshirt freshman that season, and some thought my success as a redshirt freshman the previous year had helped give the Oklahoma coaches confidence that Sam was up to the job. He sure proved it in this game. Sam calmly directed a fourth-quarter, 94-yard drive, completing several clutch third-down passes, to break a tie and win the game 28–21.

Two losses in a row!

Now I felt pressure from every angle. Going to class was bad. Walking around the campus was bad. Sitting in team meetings was bad. Everyone was irritable: the fans, the coaches, and the players. At Texas, two losses in a row was unacceptable.

I did some soul-searching by camping out in the book of James in the New Testament. The first part of James talks about trials and tribulations, which certainly fit my situation: "Consider it pure joy, my brothers and sisters, whenever you face trials of many kinds, because you know that the testing of your faith develops perseverance. Let perseverance finish its work so that you may be mature and complete, not lacking anything," James wrote (1:2–4).

Consider it pure joy? I was miserable! But I realized that everything I was doing revolved around football. All my effort and energy went into this one thing—football. Football was all

I thought about. I realized I had had become so consumed with football that my walk with Christ, my relationships with my family, my friends, and my school work were no longer a priority.

Then I read further in James: "Humble yourselves before the Lord, and he will lift you up" (4:10).

God's Word convicted me, and I knew I needed to humble myself before God and tell Him I could not do this quarterbacking thing on my own. This wasn't about winning football games; it was about turning over to the Lord everything whispered about me, all of the expectations, all of the pressures of being quarterback at the University of Texas. Then I needed to focus on being the man of God I wanted to be and continuously remind myself that without Him I was nothing.

I had strayed from that part of my relationship with God, and I had to humble myself and get my priorities straightened out. My faith in Christ had to be my top priority, followed by my family, my relationships with others, and then football. Once I recommitted myself to putting my priorities in that order, things got back on track off and on the football field.

Brad

Colt wasn't playing as well as we had hoped early in the 2007 season. I tried to coach him a bit before the Kansas State game. "You've got to pick up your end of the slack because some of your teammates are hurt," I said. "You're playing inconsistently right now, and that's on you. You have to play better."

But it wasn't long before I realized I unwittingly put more pressure on Colt, who was already feeling the stress. I knew I had to change my approach with Colt, especially after the two straight losses, so I became more of a nurturer. "You're going to get through this," I said after the loss to Oklahoma. "Everyone goes through these things. You'll come out stronger. Just keep fighting through it."

I didn't know just how much turmoil Colt was going through until later, but I was pleased to see his change in attitude. Happy quarterback, happy team. Texas went on to win five straight games, followed by an upset loss to Texas A&M on the road, before finishing the season with a big 52–34 win over tenth-ranked Arizona State in the Holiday Bowl. We all enjoyed the end-of-the-year trip to San Diego—especially Colt.

~

Colt

A month or so after our Holiday Bowl victory, a man named Johnny Polk spoke at our FCA meeting.

Johnny was the director of a big sports camp called T Bar M in New Braunfels, fifty miles southwest of Austin. He had come to put a bug in our ears about going on a sports missions trip to Peru he was organizing for spring break.

A sports missions trip? I hadn't heard of anything like that. I knew about *other* types of missions trips—like going to a Mexican orphanage to build homes or flying to a foreign country to offer medical help.

Growing up, I loved listening to Daddy Burl and GranJan's stories about their medical missions trips to Zambia. Hearing about their twenty-hour plane flight to the African continent, then the hours-long drive in the bush to reach a place called Namwianga, sounded incredible to my young ears. They also told me about how thousands of natives walked for two days just to receive medical care from their missions teams.

Daddy Burl had taught a first aid class at Abilene Christian, so he was well versed in caring for wounds and injuries. I'll never forget the story he told about meeting a poor fellow who was eaten up with leprosy—no fingers, no toes, and no ears. If he had lived in the United States, he would have been in intensive care, but he lived in the African wild, and this was the first time he'd received treatment from medical personnel.

GranJan told me how the people in Zambia lived off the land and how women carried water in old gasoline cans on their heads to their villages. There was no electricity and none of the comforts and conveniences we are used to in the United States She also told me she taught Zambian women from the Bible through an interpreter.

My grandparents made four trips to Zambia, and they told me that each one was a life-changing experience. When I got older, I wanted to go to Zambia with them, but their trips always coincided with the start of summer football practice.

By the time I got to college, the flame still burned within me to go on a missions trip. So when Johnny Polk spoke to us that night about an opportunity to go to Peru during spring break, I wanted to do it. I knew this sports missions trip could work because the timing was right—I had spring break off.

"What our team will do," he said, "is go there and teach kids how to play American sports like American football and baseball, and then we'll share our experiences with them about God and what He has done for us."

Johnny showed us pictures from past missions trips, and the images of the innocent kids touched my heart. I had never been outside of the United States—I didn't even have a passport—but the idea of getting out of my comfort zone and serving on a missions trip appealed to me. Something told me this trip would be good for my soul, especially after the tumultuous 2007 season.

"Pray about it," Johnny said to our FCA huddle group. "If you go, I promise you your life will change."

I prayed about going on the missions trip, and I felt like the

Lord was giving me nothing but green lights—except I didn't have the $1,800 it would cost to go. Most college kids, if they were in a situation like that, could simply send out letters to friends and church members, explaining their desire to go on a life-changing missions trip and seeking financial and prayer support.

But I had two problems: First, because of NCAA rules, I could not send out any kind of support letter. Second, I knew I couldn't ask Mom and Dad for the money because they didn't have it. When I explained all this to Johnny Polk, he told me he would personally ask people on my behalf for the funds to make the trip.

Johnny raised the money, but I had another obstacle to overcome: persuading Coach Brown to let me go. When I talked to him about the trip, he told me he was worried that something could happen to me in the Amazon jungle, where I'd be hours or even a day from a doctor. The other thing on his mind was that the week-long trip would be taking place during spring football practice. At Texas, the football team practiced for two weeks, got a week off for spring break, then came back for one more week of practice.

Yet Coach Brown understood the indelible impression that such a trip could make on me. "As long as you don't miss any practices, I don't see why you can't go," he said. "I think it will be good for you."

After our practice on the Friday before the start of spring break, our group of twenty—the only UT football player to join me was John Gold, our punter—took off for Lima, Peru. After our arrival in Lima, we boarded another flight, this one to Iquitos, a city of nearly four hundred thousand located in the Amazon rainforest. Iquitos has the distinction as being the largest city in the world that cannot be reached by a road. You can only get there by air or by boat.

Upon landing, we spent the night at Camp Amazon, a camping

and retreat facility just outside Iquitos. The next morning we jumped on a bus that took us into the jungle, where we boarded motorboats that took us up one of the tributaries of the mighty Amazon River. Then we traveled for about an hour on muddy roads to the small village where parents from around the area had sent their children, about two hundred in all, to attend the Christian sports camp.

When we arrived at the camp, dozens of little kids ran up and greeted us. They all wanted to play with us—throw or kick a ball of some sort—in the blazing heat and humidity.

We'd all brought our own tents and sleeping bags, and we set them up at the perimeter of the village. There was no running water, but there was an open trench in the jungle that served as a latrine if you had to pop a squat. We took our showers by standing underneath a tub of water and pulling a string to dump the water us. (Or you could step outside and get wet; it once rained for twenty hours straight while we were there.)

The people in that part of the world speak Spanish and Quechua, so when we mingled with the kids and the adults, there were always interpreters with us to help bridge the language barrier. We ate what they ate—white sticky rice. Sometimes eggs would be mixed in, but rice was their main form of sustenance. We had brought some provisions with us, but out of respect for the locals, we did not eat those foods when the kids were around.

My "job" that week was to teach the kids how to play American football. They had no clue how to play the game, so it took me and my translator a while to explain that you could either run or pass the ball, and that once your knee hits the ground, you are "down."

We started with the fundamentals, like how to hold the football when you throw it and how to catch the ball—making sure to watch the ball into your hands.

I had a blast with the kids, who ranged in age from eight to around fourteen years old. They loved to tackle each other. By the end of the week, we lined up and played a game that strongly resembled football, but we played two-hand touch.

Two things struck me about my time in the Amazon rainforest:

1. These kids didn't know me from Adam. I *loved* that. I could have gone to a sports camp in the States, and everyone would have known that I was the University of Texas quarterback. Instead, I went to Peru, where the kids had never even heard of college football—or even cared about the game. For the first time in a year and a half, I was anonymous again, and that was very freeing.

2. The way these kids worshipped God put me to shame. In the evenings, we'd hold a worship services, and the kids would jump, dance, cry, and praise God. They'd grab sticks and beat a wall or shake tambourines, uninhibited in their act of worshipping the Lord of lords.

At times I would catch myself crying at the worship services, saying to myself, *How come I can't be like that? Why can't I worship like that?* Back home we'd sit on our hands, scared to sing. But here kids almost screamed out the words to hymns and praise songs.

I decided to loosen up. I didn't know their language, so I had no idea what the kids were singing, but I hopped in and sang what I could pick up. I yelled, jumped, danced, and cried right with them—and enjoyed some of the best worship I had ever been a part of.

I thanked God for prompting me to decide to go to Peru—and for allowing me to see this place and make an impact here. When our time was over, I left most of my clothing and shoes behind, as well as ten pounds I had lost from eating rice three meals a day. I later joked to my friends that I would never eat rice again.

We spent our last evening enjoying a little R & R in Iquitos before our departure the following morning. Iquitos is a teeming city of nearly a half-million residents, so there were markets and bazaars to poke around that night.

As we walked through a market area, someone spotted a bar/restaurant called the Yellow Rose of Texas. The sign outside the place was printed in English.

"Could be interesting," someone said. "Let's check it out."

When our group of twenty walked in, it was like being transported to downtown Austin. The restaurant décor was burnt orange, a steer head dominated the main room, and the waitresses wore UT cheerleading outfits. Texas football memorabilia and photos covered the walls. It was *all* Texas.

The owner approached our group, and when he spotted me, his knees buckled. It was like he had seen a ghost.

"Co-co-colt?" he stammered.

I decided to have a little fun with him and gave him a *Who me?* look, and everyone cracked up. The owner introduced himself as Gerald Mayeaux, and he explained that he was a UT grad who had come to Peru to work in the oil business. After marrying a Peruvian woman, he opened up this bar/restaurant, the world's southernmost shrine to Texas football.

"You must sit down," he said to our group. "Please, you are my guests."

And that was the start of an amazing evening. As I sat inside the Yellow Rose of Texas, I thought about how I had left Austin and traveled to Iquitos, Peru, where no one knew me, and suddenly, out of nowhere, we walk into this bar and make this Texas Longhorns fan's day. The entire experience was funny, and a great way to end our trip.

Brad

Debra and I enjoyed hearing Colt's story about the Yellow Rose of Texas, as well as what he and his team did for the kids during their missions trip to Peru. He told us he had never seen kids so poor, kids who had absolutely nothing except for the shirts on their backs and the shorts around their waists. But he also told us they were the happiest people he had ever met. Compared with what we have back home, he said, they had nothing, but to them, what they had was everything.

"I will never, ever complain about anything again," he told us.

Going to Peru refined Colt's outlook on life and what's really important, something he needed after what had happened during the 2007 football season.

Colt

We arrived back in Austin on a Saturday night. I slept like a rock in my own bed that night, and on Sunday night I attended a team dinner. It was interesting listening to the "What I did on spring break" conversations around the table.

Which beach did you go to?

We were at South Padre Island, and we partied all week.

You should have checked out the scene in Destin. Nothing but girls and bikinis!

Then came the question about what I had done the previous week: "Hey, Colt, what did you do over spring break?"

"Ha! I went to the beach, too," I said. "The *Amazon* beach."

And so I told them about my trip to Peru. My teammates enjoyed the stories, especially the part about the Yellow Rose of Texas.

Gerald Mayeaux made a pilgrimage to a UT game the following fall, and I made arrangements for him and Johnny Polk to get tickets. I imagine how Gerald thought he had died and gone to heaven, attending a game at Memorial Stadium.

The following spring, I returned to Iquitos with Johnny Polk's team, and it was great seeing the kids again. They all remembered us, and some of the counselors had discovered what I had done on the football field over the previous year (2008) when they went to Internet shops and Googled my name.

My second visit to Iquitos wouldn't have been complete without a stop at the Yellow Rose of Texas. Gerald had really outdone himself since the last time I visited his establishment. He had commissioned a huge painting of me and the Texas offense getting ready to start a play during a game.

Gerald explained that he had taken a photo at the game he attended in Austin and later asked a Peruvian artist to reproduce it in a painting. He also had a copy of the painting made, which he wanted to give me. His thoughtfulness touched me, and now I had an extra item to check for the flight home.

I also brought home some awesome memories of Peru that remain with me to this day. As I left South America that second time, I went with this thought:

It's not about what I did for these kids but what they did for me.

CHAPTER 12

COLLEGE GRANT

Colt

Even though we finished strong and won a bowl game to go 10–3 in 2007, Coach Brown didn't want a repeat of what happened that season, so he addressed the issue before the start of summer practice.

"This season needs to be special," he told the team. "I want each one of you to make this season personally noteworthy by dedicating this year to someone close to you. Every time the going gets tough, you'll think about the person you're playing for this season."

Coach met individually with each player that summer to talk about his challenge. I decided to dedicate the 2008 season to my first cousin, Grant Hinds, who had died five months earlier under mysterious circumstances.

Though I was five years younger than Grant, we were pretty close as we were growing up. When he lived with my other cousins in Abilene, he'd spend a lot of time at our house, where we'd play catch, ride around on four-wheelers, or go fishing. Since Grant was older, I looked up to him and was his sidekick when I was in elementary school.

After Grant reached high school, I saw him a lot less—usually twice a year at family reunions or important family events. He joined the United States Marine Corps after graduating from high school and went off to war, serving three tours in Iraq and Afghanistan. I can only imagine what that was like. He was part of the second Tank Battalion, so he witnessed lots of death and destruction. One time, shortly after the U.S. invasion of Iraq in 2003, a rocket-propelled grenade hit Grant's tank, called *Devil's Advocate*.

The grenade ricocheted from the tank's open turret and into the tank, killing Grant's friend, Corporal Bernard Gooden.

Grant was injured in another firefight, but he was patched up, and the Marines sent him back to the Middle East. When he returned to the States, he battled PTSD—post-traumatic stress disorder—as well as nightmares and depression. Grant was trying to get his life back together when he enrolled at Kennesaw State University in Georgia. Even though he was struggling mentally, he was making good grades. Then he was involved in a car accident one day but did not seek medical attention. The following day, he was discovered dead on his couch in his apartment. An autopsy revealed Grant had died in his sleep from a brain hemorrhage. He was only twenty-five years old.

When my grieving aunt went to Grant's apartment to sort through his personal effects, she retrieved a football I had signed from the fireplace mantle. Aunt Sandy told me that whenever his buddies would come over, he'd show them the ball and tell everyone that I played quarterback for the University of Texas. "That's my cousin," he'd say with pride.

When I sat down with Coach Brown in his office the summer before the 2008 season, I told him, "I'm going to dedicate this year to my cousin Grant, who died a few months ago. Grant was one of my favorite cousins and served our country in Iraq and Afghanistan. He was a leader, a high-character guy, and I'm going to do everything the way he would have done it. In honor of his memory, I'm going to play my heart out for him."

Coach was moved nearly to tears at what I had told him.

Other than my parents and Coach Brown, the only other person who knew about my decision was Aunt Sandy. Because she was a divorced mom, Grant's death had been extremely hard on her. Grant was her only son, her baby boy. She was deeply moved when I told her I would be dedicating the upcoming season to his memory.

A week after I told her about my decision, Aunt Sandy called me back. Choking back tears, she said, "There's something I want to send you. Grant was wearing a crucifix when he passed away, and I want you to have it."

Aunt Sandy mailed me his silver crucifix. Every time I suited up on game day, I slipped the chain and Grant's cross over my head and around my neck before putting on my shoulder pads. That crucifix was a visible reminder that I was playing for something bigger than myself—I was also playing for my cousin Grant. "This game is for you, Grant," I'd say as I put the silver chain around my neck. "I want to play with the same heart and courage that you showed when you fought for us."

Then I'd look at the photograph of Grant in his formal Marine dress uniform. I knew he would be watching, and I wanted to give him a good effort. I wore his crucifix only during our games.

We started the 2008 campaign strong with five big wins before our Red River Rivalry date with Oklahoma. The Sooners were blazing a trail and were ranked No. 1 in the nation, but we beat them convincingly in Dallas that day, 45–35. Now we were back atop the BCS polls, and 2008 was shaping up to be the special year Coach Brown had asked it to be.

The meat of our schedule was coming up, though. One week after we beat Oklahoma, eleventh-ranked Missouri came to Austin, followed by No. 8 Oklahoma State the following week. We won both games and were looking good, averaging 48 points a game on the season.

And then we lost our perfect season by inches—maybe by half an inch.

If you're a Texas fan, you know what game I'm talking about: No. 1 Texas versus No. 7 Texas Tech, two 8–0 undefeated teams playing a big game with BCS implications. We would be playing in Lubbock, where the Texas Tech crowd would be loud and the atmosphere hostile.

When we fell behind 19–0 in the second quarter, Tech fans smelled blood in the water. Nothing very good happened for us until the third quarter, when Jordan Shipley's nifty 45-yard punt return for a touchdown got us back in the game. We were still down 22–13, however.

Then I threw an interception that Tech ran back for a touchdown, and the Red Raiders' 29–13 lead looked insurmountable. "That one's on me," I told my teammates, but I continued to encourage them—and myself—that we could still get the job done.

We made a crazy comeback that included a 91-yard touchdown pass, but it wasn't until we put together a clutch drive late in the fourth quarter that we earned our first lead: 33–32 with 1:29 to go. It was a classic eleven-play drive in which we moved the ball 80 yards in four minutes. If we could have held on for just another 89 seconds, that dramatic touchdown drive would be on the lips of Texas fans to this day.

Turns out we held on for 88 seconds.

All we needed to do was slow the Texas Tech offense down long enough to run out the clock before the Raiders could get into field goal range. But when Tech's Jamar Wall spurted past our kick-off team for a 38-yard return on the kickoff, I buried my head in a towel. Then my heart skipped a beat when we missed what looked like a sure interception off a tipped ball.

The deciding moment of the game came with eight seconds to go. Texas Tech was on our 28-yard line, meaning a field goal attempt would be 45 yards—far from a sure thing.

Texas Tech wanted to get closer. Perhaps the Raiders would throw a short pass to the middle of the field and then use their last timeout. Instead, Red Raider quarterback Graham Harrell threw a long, risky pass across the field toward the right sideline. This was our side of the field, and the play happened right in front of me.

We had double coverage on Harrell's intended receiver, Michael Crabtree. I still don't know how the ball got into Crabtree's hands, but when our guys lunged for the interception and missed, Crabtree caught the ball at the 5-yard line, made a nifty spin move, kept his balance, and tiptoed up the sideline. Only one second was left on the clock when he stepped into the end zone.

TV cameras then showed me, helmet off, with a look of utter disbelief on my face. At first we thought Crabtree might have stepped on the sideline, but the replay official verified that the Tech receiver had stayed in bounds. When the verdict went against us, our perfect season went up in smoke.

It was the most shocking ending to a game that I'd ever been a part of. It's still hard to believe that the game ended that way, but it did. The 39–33 defeat stung even worse because we had fought and clawed our way back into a game that looked like a lost cause. We had victory in our grasp, only to lose in the last possible second. The loss dropped us to No. 4 in the polls, setting up quite a BCS controversy at the end of the season.

This is difficult to explain, but when Oklahoma blew out Texas Tech 65–21 three weeks later, it created a three-way tie in the Big 12 South Division between Texas, Texas Tech, and Oklahoma. According to tiebreaker rules, when three teams finish with the same conference record, the team ranked highest in the BCS rankings on December 1 goes to the Big 12 championship game. The tiebreaker went to Oklahoma, which, according to the BCS computer, finished one spot ahead of us at No. 2, meaning the Sooners would get the chance to play Missouri for the Big 12 title.

Just like that, we were out of the Big 12 championship game *and* the BCS national championship picture, which was all the more frustrating because we had beaten Oklahoma by 10 points at a neutral site and creamed Missouri in Austin, 56–31. Yet those two teams were playing for the Big 12 title.

I was so disappointed that I didn't want to watch the Oklahoma–Missouri game. I decided instead to go deer hunting with a friend in Throckmorton, which is located about thirty-five miles west of my parents' home in Graham.

I traveled to Mom and Dad's place on Friday night, lost in my thoughts. I knew we were the best one-loss team in the country—none of the top teams were undefeated—and I thought we deserved to play in the BCS Championship Game. The problem was that we had lost to Texas Tech at the wrong time. I vowed that I would do everthing I could not to be put in that situation the following season. I was going to work harder and make sure our team was better so that we wouldn't be sitting home while two other teams played in the next Big 12 championship game.

The next morning, I got up early and drove to my buddy's ranch just outside Throckmorton. I was still angry and frustrated that we weren't playing in the Big 12 title game. I wanted to get away from everything and everybody and forget about football for the day.

When I arrived, we prepared ourselves for a day of hunting. We started walking across his fields, rifles cradled in our arms. I was fortunate enough to get a shot at a buck that day, but my friend didn't get one. I did the field dressing. Over the years, I had become pretty good at this. Growing up on the ranch allowed a lot of experience in field dressing deer. Most people I hunted with, especially my teammates, didn't have much desire to clean the deer, so I did it.

By the time I had finished cleaning the deer, it was getting dark. We sat around a campfire and cooked hamburgers for dinner. There was something peaceful about sitting around the fire and watching the flames dance. This was what I loved to do—get away from everything and clear my mind, without having to see or talk to anybody except my friend. Believe me, I didn't go hunting that day to take out my frustration by shooting a deer. I wanted to escape the all-encompassing world of football for twenty-four hours, and I succeeded.

After we finished eating dinner, I drove back to my parents' home, where Dad had the Oklahoma-Missouri game on. I didn't want to watch any part of it, especially after Dad informed me that Oklahoma was way ahead. (We needed Missouri to win if we were to have any chance of playing in the BCS Championship Game.)

I went off to bed. The next day, I learned that Oklahoma, behind Sam Bradford, had laid down 60-plus points on Missouri—winning 62–41. The solid victory earned the Sooners the opportunity to play Tim Tebow's Florida Gators for the national championship. We were on the outside looking in, but that's how it is with the BCS computer rankings. Complaining about it did no good. We were headed toward the Fiesta Bowl and a date with Ohio State.

There was some good news though: I learned I was one of the three finalists for the Heisman Trophy. The other two were Sam Bradford and Tim Tebow. Believe it or not, I had never met either one of them before. I may have shaken hands with Sam after a Red River game, but that was about the extent of our knowledge of each other.

In mid-December, I traveled to New York City to participate in the Heisman Trophy activities—appearances, photo ops, interviews, and a lot of meet-and-greets. It was a whirlwind time but a tremendous amount of fun. Tim had made history the year before when he became the first-ever sophomore to win the coveted Heisman Trophy. Since he had been through all this before, and since he had a large contingent of family and friends with him in New York, Sam and I didn't see him that much, so we spent the majority of our time together.

It turned out Sam and I hit if off. We found out we had a lot in common. His mother was an elementary school PE teacher, just like my mother. He liked to fish; I liked to fish. He liked to play golf; I liked to play golf. We were both simple, laid-back football players who didn't need a lot of attention. I also learned that Sam was a committed Christian. I liked Sam, and after that weekend we stayed in contact by texting each other. We even got together to make an "I Am Second" evangelistic video in which we talked about the importance of having Christ in our lives.

The day before the Heisman award presentation, my parents, Chance and Case, and my grandparents Daddy Burl and GranJan flew to New York from Dallas. (My future wife, Rachel, was also there.) It was great sharing this moment with them. That evening, the Heisman folks took all three finalists and their families on a walking tour of Manhattan. It was quite a scene—a large group of two dozen people, complete with a security escort and photographers—walking around the bright lights of Times Square while tourists pointed and took pictures of us. Then they walked us over to Rockefeller Plaza, where their photographers took shots of us in front of the famous Christmas tree. We ended our tour by riding elevators to the top of Rockefeller Center, where we took in the tremendous nighttime view of Manhattan, all lit up in brilliant Christmas lights.

Brad

Walking the streets of Manhattan with several of New York's finest keeping the autograph seekers at bay was a bit surreal. Chance and Case thought it was pretty cool, and so did I.

When we were done with the walking tour, the Tebows said good-bye, leaving the Bradford and McCoy families behind. We decided to grab a bite to eat at a local grill. I sat between Colt and Debra, and across the table, Kent Bradford sat between Sam and his mom, Martha. They were good people, and we shared a memorable evening that included plenty of football stories.

On the morning of the Heisman Trophy presentation, which was set for 8:00 p.m. that night at the Nokia Theatre, Colt had to take off for more appearances. Debra, the boys and I, Rachel, and my parents walked from our hotel, the Hilton of the Americas, to Central Park. We watched the ice skaters, took pictures, ate hot dogs from the street vendors, and talked about all the movies we had seen over the years that were filmed in Central Park.

Colt

At the Heisman event, Sam, Tim, and I were waiting backstage saying things to one another like, *Hey, man, if you win, that'll be great. I'm happy for you.*

There was a great spirit among us. Just before we walked out, I said to Sam and Tim, "Hey, if either of you win, understand that you have an opportunity to give God the glory. Just remember that." (I mentioned earlier in this chapter that I had found out Sam was a committed Christian. The same was also true of Tim Tebow.)

"Yeah, you're exactly right," Tim said.

"I'm 100 percent with you," Sam agreed.

We sat together in the front row at the Heisman ceremony, all of us a bit stiff in our coats and ties, listening as commentators and past winners said nice things about us. My heart was pounding; now I knew what it was like for those singers on *American Idol.* I had some notes prepared in case I won—a few bullet points, including the notation to give God the glory—but I didn't believe I was the favorite. I thought they'd give the Heisman to Sam because (1) Tim had won it the previous year, and (2) Sam's team, Oklahoma, would be playing in the BCS Championship Game and Texas wouldn't be.

After a few speeches, Professor Sanford Wurmfeld, representing the Heisman Trust Board, announced Sam as the winner. Tim and I stood up as he graciously accepted our hugs and handshakes before making his way to the stage.

The first words out of Sam's mouth were:

"There are so many people I need to thank. There's no way I'd be here without everyone in my life. First I need to thank God. He's given me so many blessings, He's blessed me with so many opportunities, and He's put so many wonderful people in my life that I give all the credit to Him. Without Him, I'd be nowhere and we'd all be nowhere."

Great job, Sam.

I learned afterward that Sam, Tim, and I had been locked in the second closest three-man race in the seventy-three-year history of the Heisman Trophy award. Voters can vote for three players, ranking them 1-2-3. First-place votes are worth three points, second-place votes are worth two points, and third-place votes are worth one point.

Sam won with 1,726 total points, edging out my 1,604 points and Tim's 1,575. A breakdown of the voting results was very telling: I had won the Midwest region, where Sam and I play, while Tim had won the South by a large margin. But Sam won because he had run stronger than both of us in the rest of the country.

The Longhorns still had a big bowl game to play against tenth-ranked Ohio State in the Fiesta Bowl—the next to last game of the bowl season—which is played in Glendale, Arizona, a suburb of Phoenix. It turned out to be one of those "No Fear" games that I had dreamed about playing ever since I started tossing a football at Dad's football practices.

Here was the situation: We were down 21–17 with 2:05 to play, and we had the ball on our own 22-yard line. Seventy-eight yards to go, and we hadn't moved the ball much all game. This was our final chance. Down by four, a field goal wouldn't help us; we had to score a touchdown. With so little time left on the clock, we were in fourth-down territory, as they say.

We needed to make a fourth-down play during the drive. On a fourth-and-three from Ohio State's 43-yard line, I rolled out to my right and looked for receiver James Kirkendoll. James was supposed to run to first-down marker and make a quick square out. This was one of our go-to plays in fourth-and-short-yardage situations. James's job was to know where the sticks were.

I hit James just after he made his cut, and the Ohio State defense dropped him at the first down marker on the 40-yard line. It all depended on the spot, and the covering official marked the ball just inches past the first-down marker, according to the measurement. When Ohio State coach Jim Tressel demanded a booth review of the spot, we knew anything could happen. Our hearts were in our throats until the official announced that "after further review" we had made the first down.

Following that reprieve, I passed to Brandon Collins for 14 yards to take us to the Ohio State 26-yard line. There were just 27 seconds left—not much time, but we had two time outs remaining.

From the shotgun, I quickly found Quan Cosby over the middle. Two Ohio State linebackers lurched for the ball instead of for Quan, who I hit in full stride at the 23-yard line. He kept right on going, sprinting into the end zone untouched to give us the lead with 16 seconds to go.

Final score: 24–21, Texas. I was named the game's offensive most valuable player after completing 41 of 59 passes for 414 yards, a school record. What a dream ending to a 12–1 season.

I knew Grant would be proud.

Now if only something as dramatic as that would happen in the BCS Championship Game the following season. I wanted a storybook ending to my senior year at Texas, but I had no idea that a different type of ending was waiting for me.

CHAPTER 13

A CASE STUDY IN JOY AND DISAPPOINTMENT

Colt

The media loves a good "story line," and the story they created leading up to my final year of college football was that Tim Tebow's Florida, Sam Bradford's Oklahoma, and Colt McCoy's Texas would be fighting it out for the national title. THE TOP THREE QUARTER-BACKS ON THE TOP THREE TEAMS was how a *Sporting News* headline read going into the 2009 season.

Sounded good to me. Before the start of the season, I was fired up because this would be my final chance to win a national championship at Texas. We certainly had as good a chance as any school in the country. I couldn't wait for the campaign to start.

Just before 1:00 p.m. on the day before our home opener against Louisiana-Monroe, I walked over to the Moncrief-Neuhaus Athletic Center, where a sleek bus was waiting to take players to a nearby children's hospital. Several freshmen and sophomores were trailing me. I had seen them at lunch and said, "Hey, if you don't have class, let's go to the hospital."

The Dell Children's Medical Center was just a few miles north of the UT campus, and every Friday before a home game, a bus would deposit players at the front entrance. For the next hour or so, we would make the rounds, visiting brave children who were fighting life-threatening diseases such as leukemia, brain cancer, and congenital heart disease.

This would be my fifth season visiting sick children before home games. The players were not obligated to go—volunteers only—but

I thought it was important for me to be there. Not many players showed up my first couple of years at Texas, but the number had been building because my teammates saw that visiting sick children was a priority for me. By my junior year, our numbers had grown to twenty to forty Longhorn players boarding the bus on Friday afternoons to ride over to the cancer wards at Dell.

There's something about visiting terminally ill kids that hits you like a punch to the stomach. Many of these kids, bald from chemotherapy treatments and with their lonely eyes set deep in their sockets, were looking death straight in the eye. I can remember visiting with certain kids one week and returning the following week to find their rooms empty—they had died in the interim. Visiting the sick children was a very emotional experience for me, and there were times when I didn't want to go. I never liked the hospital smells or the heavy pallor that hung in the hallways, but I went in the hope that my visits offered a few moments of joy to the hurting kids and their families.

Visiting these gravely ill children was also important to me because I saw it as a way to show God my appreciation for allowing me to be healthy enough to play a game I loved before millions of people. Some would say that it was a way of giving back, and there's a certain amount of truth in that. But our Friday hospital visits turned out to be a lot more than that for me. Spending time in a cancer ward taught me more lessons about life than I ever could have learned elsewhere.

No matter what the kids said or how much parents thanked me, I couldn't help but get on my knees at night and pray to God, saying, "Thank You, Lord, and help me to always be a servant to these kids. Allow me to help those kids smile and laugh. Give me the right words to say. Thank You for giving me this opportunity to do what I can for Your glory."

I think I had been given extra sensitivity to the plight of sick children when I was a ten-year-old boy. Case was around five years old at the time, and we began to notice mysterious red marks on the side of his face, his back, and his lower extremities. Mom took him to a dermatologist, who diagnosed him with an autoimmune disease known as scleroderma, the symptoms of which include thickening of the skin, spontaneous scarring, and inflammation. Scleroderma is especially rare in children and causes changes in the skin, blood vessels, muscles, and internal organs.

For the next three years or so after Case's diagnosis, we made long trips once a month to the nearest children's hospital—Texas Scottish Rite Hospital for Children in Dallas—so he could receive treatment. Those six-hour round-trip journeys on Saturdays were eye-openers, and watching Case go through painful therapies was difficult to stomach. Different spots on his body had hardened, and doctors did their best to limit the damage to his face and back.

Case's condition wasn't life-threatening, but my parents wanted to leave no stone unturned in a quest to give him a chance to grow up and live a normal life. They approved the use of several chemotherapy-like drugs, all of which took a heavy toll on his young body.

As I sat in the Scottish Rite waiting rooms, I saw scores of children who were much worse off than Case—children suffering from missing limbs to terminal cancer. Everything I saw made a profound impression on me. Here I was, healthy and strong and wanting to be an athlete someday, and then I saw what these kids and my brother had to go through. I also noted the sacrifices my parents made to get Case the best medical treatment available. Those were scary times for him and for our family, but my youngest brother showed great courage and never complained.

Back home I looked out for Case in the school yard. Children sometimes teased him and picked on him with mean taunts because he had received treatments that impacted the left side of his face. The nicest thing any of them said was, "Hey, Case. What happened? It looks like you have dirt on your face." They wouldn't say any hurtful things to him when I was around, though, because they learned quickly that they would have to deal with me if they did.

I admire the way Case has dealt with the scars on his face and on his back and lower legs. The worst parts of scleroderma are behind him now, and I see a bright future ahead. These days he's trying to follow in my footsteps as a quarterback at the University of Texas. He won the backup role behind Garrett Gilbert during the 2010 season and saw limited action during his true freshman year.

So why is Case trying to make his mark at Texas when he could have played at other top schools after a great high school career playing for my dad at Graham High?

I think the answer dates back to the day I sat down with Coach Brown in the spring of my junior year of high school and promised him, "I'm going to be a Longhorn."

Case, a sixth grader at the time, was there that day in Coach Brown's office. I think his comfort level with Coach Brown and the Texas program is one of the big reasons he accepted UT's scholarship offer on National Signing Day in early 2010. He wanted to go to Texas, and while he knew it wouldn't be easy following me, he felt like he had been part of the Longhorn family since seventh grade.

When I graduated from Texas and was drafted by the Cleveland Browns, one of the first things I did was become a spokesperson for Scott & White Healthcare, which was building a new children's hospital on Interstate 35 between Austin and Dallas to give central Texas kids a closer place to heal. I had seen firsthand the impact a children's hospital can have on surrounding communities and on families such as ours, and that's why I agreed to become part of a $50 million fund-raising project that will help Scott & White open the children's hospital in late 2011.

~

My senior season at Texas began with a home game against Louisiana-Monroe in a refurbished Darrell K Royal-Texas Memorial Stadium that had been expanded from 89,000 seats to just over 101,000 seats. Memorial Stadium was rocking when we ran out on the field.

We kept the Texas Cowboys busy firing Smokey the cannon in 2009. After drilling Louisiana-Monroe 59–10, we laid down 64 points against the University of Texas at El Paso. The week before the UTEP game, we exacted revenge on Texas Tech, winning 34–24.

I was sick with a nasty head cold all week leading up to our annual Red River game against Oklahoma. During the heated contest, I nearly lost my right thumbnail when my throwing hand hit the helmet of Oklahoma's defensive tackle Gerald McCoy. The Oklahoma defense threw every kind of blitz at me and stymied our offense.

It was one of those "winning ugly" games that featured 21 penalties and eight turnovers, including one interception I threw midway through the fourth quarter that could have given me nightmares for a long time. We were nursing a 16–13 lead, but we were on Oklahoma's 12-yard line following one of our interceptions with 7:22 to go. Score a red zone touchdown, and Oklahoma—who had lost Sam Bradford for the season earlier in the game—would be put away.

Instead, Sooner cornerback Brian Jackson intercepted my short pass and took off on what looked like a coast-to-coast touchdown that would have put Oklahoma ahead. Jackson had blockers around him with one last Longhorn in pursuit—me. I made a desperate dive and somehow tripped him up at the 30-yard line.

Then our defense came up with another interception, and it was up to the Texas offense to run the last 3:31 off the clock. I had never felt more satisfaction in grinding out a non-scoring drive, which is why—as the final seconds ticked off—I turned toward the Burnt Orange end of the Cotton Bowl and delivered a giant fist pump.

We knew we couldn't afford to lose a game if we wanted to play for the national championship, so we played with a sense of urgency all season long. We were ranked No. 3 behind unbeaten Florida and Alabama for most of the season, but that would change on Saturday, December 5, 2009, when we played Nebraska in the Big 12 championship game and Florida and Alabama squared off in the Southeastern Conference championship game. With the No. 1 and No. 2 teams playing one another, the loser would be knocked out of the BCS Championship Game. We figured if we beat Nebraska, we would move up to the No. 2 slot and earn a date in Pasadena.

Once again, a game that determined whether we would play for the national championship was decided by a single second—just like the Texas Tech game a year earlier.

No. 21–ranked Nebraska was a stubborn opponent, and it seemed like I was running for my life all game long. I had never been sacked more than four times in a game before, but the Cornhuskers took me down *nine* times, including four and a half sacks from the giant hands of Ndamukong Suh, the 307-pound defensive tackle who was in my kitchen all night. A couple of times he threw me around like a rag doll.

We trailed 12–10 following a Huskers field goal with 1:44 left to go. We hadn't moved the ball much at all, but we caught a break when the Nebraska kickoff went out of bounds, giving us possession at the 40-yard line. We caught another break when Jordan Shipley caught a 19-yard pass on first down and was horse-collared on the tackle to add another 15 yards.

Suddenly, we were within field goal range at the 26-yard line, but Suh dropped me for a two-yard loss. I tried a quarterback keeper on the next play but lost a yard, putting us on the 29-yard line, meaning that our kicker, Hunter Lawrence, would face a do-or-die 46-yard field goal attempt. That was right on the edge of Hunter's range, and we knew that getting five yards closer in this situation would bolster his confidence.

Meanwhile, the clock was running . . . 27 seconds . . . 24 seconds . . . it was third down . . . we still had a timeout left. We could have let the clock run down and gone for the field goal, but we called a play to squeeze out a few more yards.

We were in a no-huddle offense. The play the coaches signaled in called for a mirror route, which meant the passing play could be run to the right or left side of the field, depending on the strength of the defensive formation. Our code word was *Rita* for the right side and *Linda* to the left. I started yelling, "Rita, Rita," to the offense, but the crowd was insanely loud, causing us momentary confusion about which side we were going to.

Meanwhile, the clock was moving . . . 10 seconds, 9 . . . .

We had to get the ball snapped. With seven seconds to go, the ball was in my hands.

I rolled to my right, which ate up a few more precious seconds. I didn't like what I saw, and I knew I had to get rid of the football to stop the clock. I tossed the ball out of bounds.

I was knocked down as I threw, and suddenly Cornhusker players were running jubilantly around me, celebrating. *Celebrating?* That's when I realized something horrible must have happened. The scoreboard clock showed :00, meaning time had run out.

A sickening feeling came to my stomach, but I knew this couldn't be right. I was sure we had one or two seconds left.

Coach Brown held up a single digit to the officials, arguing that we had a second left. The referee signaled that the game wasn't over, which didn't go over well with the Nebraska bench. The play went straight to review, and the booth official superimposed the clock over the replay of my pass and saw that the ball had clearly hit out of bounds with one second to go.

What a difference one tick of the clock makes.

Hunter Lawrence, who had never kicked a game-winning field goal for Texas, jogged out onto the field. His holder was Jordan Shipley, who whispered encouraging Bible verses after Nebraska called timeout to "ice" our kicker. From the left hash mark, Hunter kicked the 46-yarder just inside the left goal post, and then it was our turn to run onto the field to celebrate.

Hindsight is always 20/20, and looking back, we should have used our last timeout when the play clock got under 10 seconds. But, as they say on *American Idol*, this is "live TV." Crazy stuff happens in football, and just when you think you've seen it all, something new occurs.

It felt great to win and remain undefeated. Back in July, Coach Brown had told the media, "Obviously, the only thing Colt wants is to be one second better."

Coach Brown was right. In my mind, the one-second monkey was off our backs, and now we were freed up to play in college football's biggest game—the BCS Championship Game at the Rose Bowl in Pasadena, California.

Waiting for us was Alabama, which had humbled Tim Tebow's Florida Gators 32–13.

I heard the Crimson Tide looked really good.

∿

Following the Nebraska game, I learned that I was one of five finalists for the Heisman Trophy. I made the return trip with my folks to New York City, where we watched the trophy be handed to Mark Ingram, the Alabama running back who was figured to be the favorite.

Then it was back to Austin for more preparation for Alabama. Before boarding the team charter to the West Coast, though, I handed in my last paper, took my last final, and graduated from the University of Texas. It was kind of anticlimactic because I did not walk with my class in a cap and gown. My major was sports management, and I ended up with a 3.4 grade point average—a mixture of As and Bs that I was happy with, especially given the time commitment expected of me to play football at the University of Texas.

∼

Everything about the BCS Championship Game felt right and comfortable to me. I loved it that two of the most storied programs in college football would be playing for the national championship trophy. We would be taking on No. 1–ranked Alabama in the Rose Bowl, and I had good vibes from the last time we played in that historic stadium. Who could forget Vince Young's dash to the end zone on a fourth-and-five to beat USC?

Coach Brown gave a great pep talk before we took the field. "You've heard all week long that you're not good enough to win this game," he bellowed. "I'm telling you that we're more ready for this game than any game we've prepared for this season. This game is ours!"

The seniors and everyone else on this team were pumped up and ready. We were the underdogs, but we didn't care. We knew we were going to win, plain and simple.

I don't think I had ever been so keyed up as I was when I ran onto the Rose Bowl field with the rest of my teammates a few minutes before the opening kickoff. I stood on the sideline and took in the pregame pageantry. Up above, the United States Air Force Academy parachute jumpers, the Wings of Blue, soared into the bowl-shaped stadium with yellow and red smoke trailing from canisters around their ankles. Then singer Josh Groban performed the National Anthem, giving me goose bumps. That was topped off by four F-18 Super Hornets rocking the stadium crowd of 94,906 people with their fly-by. I fought back tears because I knew this was it—my final game in a Texas uniform.

As one of the four co-captains, I walked to midfield for the ceremonial coin toss by Keith Jackson, the legendary ABC college football announcer. I had grown up hearing him say, "Whoa, Nellie!" after a great play he'd just witnessed.

Alabama won the coin toss, and the Tide elected to receive. They took our kickoff to their 33-yard line, and after that good things started happening for us. A stop, a false start, a sack, and an incomplete pass gave Alabama a fourth-and-23 from its own 20-yard line.

You'd think that after such as inauspicious start, the 'Bama punter would just kick the ball as far as he could and give his defense a chance to establish some control. But no, P. J. Fitzgerald faked a punt and tossed a woefully short and ill-advised pass that was easy pickings for our safety Blake Gideon.

We were in business on the Alabama 37-yard line. We moved down to the 16-yard line in four plays, and coming up was an option play. After taking the snap, I had the choice of flipping the ball to my trailing tailback, Tre' Newton, or trying to get some yards on my own.

The play quickly broke down as I moved to my left. I got hit from behind, and a shiver of pain ran through my shoulder. It wasn't a sharp pain, but I definitely felt it in my right shoulder. The blow sent me falling to the ground, and I landed on the back of my center, Chris Hall. Then I bounced right back up because we had another play to run. (I didn't even know who hit me, but I learned it was Marcell Dareus, Alabama's 6-foot, 3-inch, 296-pound defensive end.)

Something felt funny in my throwing arm. Not any intense pain, but more like no feeling at all—a numbness. I tried moving my arm a bit, and that's when I knew something was not right. Instead of returning to the huddle, I started jogging toward the Texas sideline. Using my left arm, I motioned for Coach Brown to replace me. My right arm was useless, and a sinking feeling filled the pit of my stomach.

I got down on one knee while the Texas trainers tended to me. Meanwhile, my backup, Garrett Gilbert, a true freshman who had only played at the end of a few blowouts, had to come in.

"Can you move your arm?" one of the trainers asked.

"I can, but my arm feels numb," I answered.

I rotated my shoulder, but it was clear something was wrong.

"We need to get an X-ray," said one of the trainers.

The trainers escorted me on a long walk off the field and into the tunnel leading to the visitors' locker room. On the way, they discussed whether I had broken my shoulder blade or collarbone.

I took off my uniform and shoulder pads for the X-ray. While we waited for the results, the trainers asked me if I could hold out my right arm and keep it up. I couldn't do that; my arm lacked the strength to stay level. Then I was asked to push against the hands of one of the trainers. I had no power.

"You've obviously lost strength in the arm," said a trainer. "This could be really bad and you're done for the night, or you could get your strength back within the hour."

I laid down on a trainer's table. I was mentally processing what

I had just heard when I glanced over and saw my father walk into the locker room. He had a grim look on his face. Dad had never come into my locker room during a game, so I knew this had to be serious.

Brad

When Colt went down, Debra and I began praying that God would enable him to keep playing. When we realized that wasn't going to happen and Colt was led off the field, I wanted to see what was going on, so I told Debra and my parents I was heading to the locker room. Fortunately, I saw a team official who guided me past security.

When I walked into the locker room, I saw Colt lying prone on a trainer's table, shoulder pads off, and tears on his face.

"Dad, I had 'em," he said. "I knew everything they were going to do before they did it. I know we could win this game."

I tried to console him and be optimistic. When he said he was experiencing numbness in his arm, I replied that maybe it would go away.

Colt pulled himself up. He wanted to see if he could throw a little. Perhaps his arm strength had returned.

I stepped about 10 yards away from Colt and asked him to toss me the football. In the back of my mind, I could see a little boy asking me to play catch in the front yard, and the emotions of the moment hit me in the chest.

This time, though, Colt threw like he was using his left hand. The ball fluttered with no zip. After the second and third wobbly pass, I knew his college football career was over.

More emotions, including disappointment, swept over me.

This wasn't the ending any of us would have scripted.

Colt

When I threw the ball to Dad, I had no idea where it was going. I could feel all my fingers except for my thumb. My arm felt like a wet noodle. I wasn't in pain, but my arm was dead.

The trainer told me I probably had a pinched nerve in my shoulder. All we could do was put ice on my shoulder and see if it would respond.

I kept an eye on the game on a TV set hanging in the corner. It wasn't looking good for us. The Crimson Tide had rolled to a 24–6 lead as the first half came to an end. I witnessed a dispirited bunch of Longhorns walking into the locker room.

Coach Brown told the team assembled around him that I wouldn't be coming back. I then asked if I could say a few words. I told the team they would have to rally around our backup quarterback. "Offensive line, you have to block for Garrett and make it easy for him," I said. "Garrett, you find the open guy. Don't think about this as anything else but practice. Defense, if you can hold them, we have a chance. If you let them keep pounding the running game and let them keep running the clock, we don't have a chance. You need to rally around each other, rally around Garrett. Let's go win this thing."

That's all I could do. I added that I was going to stay in my uniform and be on the sidelines in the second half to support the team. I refused to put my arm in a sling because I didn't want to call any more attention to myself.

I did what I could to mentor Garrett in the second half. I wore a headset to stay involved with the play-calling and signaled to him some things I was seeing. Garrett picked up his passing and led a remarkable comeback. We pulled within 24–21 with 6:15 to go, but Alabama won going away, 37–21, to claim the national championship.

After congratulating several Alabama players, I walked back toward the locker room, downcast as confetti swirled in the air for the victors. I felt a tug on my left arm. It was Lisa Salters, the Texas sideline reporter for ABC. A cameraman was next to her.

"Colt, do you have a minute?" Lisa asked me.

I didn't think I had a choice. The next thing I heard was Lisa saying, "I'm with Texas quarterback Colt McCoy. Colt, what was it like for you to watch this game—the last game in uniform—from the sideline?"

I ruefully shook my head. Her question jump-started all sorts of conflicting emotions within me. I knew Lisa and the national TV audience were waiting for me to say something were—something profound.

I started to answer twice, stammering, "I . . . I . . ." before stopping to compose myself. I said a quick prayer. Then I took another long moment to gather myself before I delivered my answer.

"I . . . I love this game. I have a passion for this game. I've done everything I can to contribute to my team, and we made it this far. It's unfortunate that I didn't get to play. I would have given everything I had to be out there with my team. Congratulations to Alabama. I love the way our team fought. Garrett Gilbert stepped in and played as good as he could play. He did a tremendous job. I always give God the glory. I never question why things happen the way they do. God is in control of my life, and I know that if nothing else, I am standing on the Rock."

I left the Rose Bowl field having no idea what I'd just said.

Brad

After the game was over, Debra and I and Colt's grandparents remained in our seats. We couldn't move. We were mesmerized by what we had just witnessed. When Garrett Gilbert threw two touchdown passes and got Texas back into the game, the crowd was chanting, "Gilbert, Gilbert," on a night when the stage was set for Colt.

We knew it would be awhile before Colt came out of the locker room because of all the interviews he'd have to do. So we sat there until there was no one left in the Rose Bowl except for those cleaning up the trash. The ushers came by and asked us to go, but quite honestly, we did not leave the first time they asked us.

About an hour after the game, we made our way toward the Texas dressing room. We found a team official who let Debra and me into the locker room. Colt was still being treated, but we were able to have a few moments with him. We told our son that we'd see him back at the team hotel.

It was after midnight by the time we hiked two miles to our car, battled LA traffic, and reached our hotel. The team had beaten us to the hotel because they had a police escort. We found Colt in his room, unwinding from the emotional evening. He was reading a devotional that contained the following words:

> My certainty must be stronger than my doubt. The battle is won before I ever start the fight. I choose faith over fear. As Jeremiah stated, "Blessed is the man who trusts in the Lord."

Debra and I were moved to tears that Colt would seek spiritual inspiration at such a low moment in his life. He showed amazing maturity.

Debra dabbed at the moisture from her eyes. "You know, you really handled yourself well tonight," she said.

"Thanks, Mom," Colt replied. "It means a lot to hear you say that."

I decided to check my cell phone for voice messages. I had several dozen, many more than usual. I listened to a couple from friends saying they had seen Colt on TV after the game and that they wanted me to know that what he said was awesome.

"Son, what did you say in that postgame interview on TV?" I asked.

"I don't know, Dad," Colt said. "I really don't remember what I said. All I remember is that the reporter asked me a question, and I prayed that God would supply me with the right answer."

Over the next twenty-four hours, it seemed like my phone blew up from all the texts and voice messages from friends, family members, preachers, and pastors—all praising the amazing statement that Colt had made about "standing on the Rock." Even today, when I meet someone the first time, that person will often say something like, "I remember what your son said after the Rose Bowl game."

Where God closed a door—winning the national championship—He opened up another one. His interview with Lisa Salters has been viewed nearly three hundred thousand times on YouTube and has given us a great story to share when Colt and I speak in public. People heard Colt give God the glory, even in defeat. They heard a visibly disappointed Colt say that he wouldn't question the God who was in control of his life. Finally, millions heard Colt say that he was standing on the Rock, a wonderful reminder to others that we can trust in the Lord no matter what happens.

Colt

In question-and-answer times when I speak, people sometimes ask me where that last statement came from. ("God is in control of my life, and I know that if nothing else, I am standing on the Rock.")

Before the start of the 2009 season, I started keeping a journal. A couple of times a week, I would write down thoughts that struck me after I had read scripture, or I would record things I had experienced. Sometimes I would write down helpful stories I had heard or read. Keeping a journal helped me share my experiences and these stories when I was asked to speak at FCA meetings, youth events, business conferences, or church conventions.

On the eve of the national championship game against Alabama, I was reading my Bible in my hotel room before falling asleep, which was my custom. I was reading in Isaiah when I came across these words: "Trust in the LORD forever, for the LORD, the LORD himself, is the Rock eternal" (26:4).

Looking back, I wasn't thinking about that verse as I left the Rose Bowl field. I was thinking about how we had just lost, how my college football career was over, when Lisa Salters set the microphone before me and gave me a national pulpit. Suddenly, I had to switch gears. I was keenly aware that I was on national TV and that millions were looking in. That's why I took my time, searching for the right answer.

After hesitating twice, I knew I had to say something, so I just started talking. What came out surprised even me. Today I believe the Holy Spirit gave me the right words to say in defeat.

Since that evening, I can't tell you the number of people who've stopped me on the street or in airports and thanked me for the graciousness I displayed and the spiritual truth I shared that evening. I just smile and express my gratitude.

But I must be honest here: for the first week or so after my shoulder injury, my faith was rocked.

Why did this have to happen? I asked the Lord in my prayer time. *Why did You let this happen at this moment, after all I have gone through, after the way I've lived for You? You know what I stand for. You know how important this game was to me.*

God did speak back to me, not in an audible voice, but through

His Word. I started reading the Old Testament book of Job, which describes how the man Job remained faithful to God, even after he had lost his family, his wealth, and his health.

As I read, I realized how foolish I had been to question anything God does, especially on a football field. You see, God doesn't care about football. He doesn't care how many games I win or lose. I realized that in the grand scheme of things, I'm a nobody. I need God way more than God needs me to win football games.

Then I started thinking about those kids in Peru who struggle to get more than one meal of white rice a day, who lack clean drinking water. I started thinking of those kids at Dell Children's Medical Center who are dealing with a cancer diagnosis and a bleak future. I started thinking about families who struggle to keep a roof over their heads or who don't have enough warm clothes and enough to eat.

And I was complaining to God about getting hurt in a football game?

God taught me an important lesson, and it was this: " 'For my thoughts are not your thoughts, neither are your ways my ways,' declares the LORD" (Isaiah 55:8).

I learned that we're all going to go through some tough times, and we're all going to have things happen to us that we don't want to have happen. But when those things happen to me, my job is to pick myself up, keep pressing ahead, and continue to trust in the Lord.

I had a strong feeling that as I left college football and sought to play professional football in the NFL, my trust in God would be tested again. But that was still a ways off.

There was something more urgent at that time: the diamond ring burning a hole in my pocket.

CHAPTER 14

THE PROPOSAL

Colt

We didn't have any girls living in the McCoy household as I was growing up; it was just four guys and poor Mom. Sure, my mother lent a feminine touch, but I basically grew up in a world of testosterone.

Like most boys, I thought all girls had cooties when I was in elementary school. Dad was happy that I was a lot more interested in sports than in girls back then. But he knew there would come a time when I would grow taller and stronger, my voice would change, I'd get hair on my legs and under my arms, and hormones would change my feelings toward girls and I'd actually be *attracted* to them.

When I was twelve or so, Dad said he wanted to take me on a hunting trip—just the two of us. I remember Mom giving us a sly smile as we left the house.

The next morning, we were sitting in our blind, waiting for the deer to make their appearance, when Dad began speaking casually. "Son, I know you've grown up around the locker room," he began, "and I know you've heard things about girls and about sex from the guys. Some of what they say is true and some of what they say couldn't be further from the truth. It's time we talked about some of these things, which is why I wanted to take you on this hunting trip."

So Dad and I talked about girls and sex—although the way I remember it, he did most of the talking and I did most of the listening. The gist of what he said was that a guy's attraction to the female body is a natural, God-given desire, and that once I hit full-blown adolescence, it would be natural for me to want to hang around girls. Very soon, he explained, I'd find a girl's beauty tugging at my eyes for attention.

The temptation, he said, is to go beyond a natural and normal look. "Real men understand this," Dad said, "and real men can handle it. I know who you want to become, which is why I'm encouraging you to be willing to wait. Marriage and sex are a gift from God, and that is how it's supposed to be."

Dad had a lot more to say about the temptations all men go through, but he emphasized that God had created a right time and place for sex, and that was within marriage. "I'm just telling you, it's going to be tough to wait," he said. "It's going to be unpopular, but that's how God wants us to live. It's in the Bible; it's in His Word."

Dad also warned me about the temptations of pornography, which had become a lot easier to access around that time due to the invention of the Internet. (This conversation took place in the late 1990s, when the World Wide Web was just starting to make its way into people's homes. When my parents bought our first home computer, they put it in the master bedroom and controlled access to the Internet with a password, which allowed them to closely monitor my use.)

I dated some in high school, and I had a high school girlfriend that I continued dating during my first year of college, but our relationship faded. I then went out on a few dates with two or three different girls at UT, but nothing ever reached the "serious" stage.

Then I had those notes passed under my door at Jester East from girls basically offering me their bodies. To this day, I believe the Lord protected me from these temptations, thanks in large part to the prayers of others. I also knew that athletes, especially those in high-profile positions like starting quarterback, were subject to closer scrutiny and were held to a higher standard in many ways. That is why I was careful about my behavior with regard to drugs and alcohol, as well as with women and sex. I wanted to stay away from all of that.

Now, did I hang out with some friends and stay out late and go to a party every now and then? Yeah, I did. But I knew where not to go and I knew what my boundaries were. I never crossed those lines with alcohol, drugs, or premarital sex.

So keep this background in mind as I describe how I met and fell in love with Rachel, the young woman who would become my wife.

I first saw Rachel as she stood among a dozen or so reporters holding microphones and interviewing me after a summer practice before my junior season. She introduced herself as Rachel Glandorf, and she said she was interning at KEYE Channel 42, Austin's CBS affiliate. She was doing some on-camera work and filing a few stories. With her long blonde hair, strikingly good looks, beautiful eyes, and athletic body, she certain stood out among the grubby guys peppering me with the same old questions about how practice went and whether we could win the national championship in 2008.

Each time I was interviewed en masse after practice, Rachel stood there with the rest of the media, and I wondered, *How can I get in contact with her? How can I ever talk to her?*

With all those other journalists around, I knew I couldn't show interest in her, so I made small talk, asking her questions like "Where are you from?" She replied that she was from Waco, about ninety miles north of Austin, where she attended Baylor University.

Just from our short interactions, I knew she had definitely pushed my attraction buttons. Despite my most charming smiles, though, she appeared to have no interest in me. Of course, her coyness made me want to get to know her all the more. Rachel didn't know it at the time, but playing hard to get was exactly what I wanted.

I began thinking about what I could do to get her phone number. I couldn't ask for it with all those snoopy reporters around. But then I got my break. One day in the locker room, one of my teammates, Daniel Orr, heard me talking about Rachel. He casually mentioned that they had become Facebook "friends." (He didn't actually know Rachel. He had seen her at our practices and, on a lark, he found her profile on Facebook and asked her to friend him, and she clicked yes.)

That was my opening. One day when Daniel was at my apartment, I asked him if we could go to his Facebook page. He said yes, and I found her e-mail address and sent her a message:

> Hey, I know you are friends with Daniel, but I don't
> know how else to get ahold of you because when I see
> you, I can't ask for your phone number in front of all
> the media. I know you're busy with your job, and I'm
> real busy with football. But I would love to hang out
> and get to know you. Here's my number . . . .
> Colt.

I typed in my cell number and let my message fly into cyberspace.

I didn't hear back from Rachel right away. A week or so passed with zero response. Meanwhile, as the season approached, I kept seeing her after practice. Nothing in her eyes acknowledged that she had heard from me.

Two or three weeks later, my heart skipped a beat when I received this e-mail from Rachel:

> Hey, Colt. I usually don't respond to messages from
> people I don't know. But I guess I can make an
> exception since I stuck a microphone in your face a

few times. I am only here for the summer, but I can
probably find a time to hang out. Here's my number,
and I NEVER give it out like this, so be careful with it.

And then she typed out her phone number.

To be honest, because of the delayed response *and* because Daniel knew about my interest in Rachel, I wondered if the e-mail was from him or one of his buddies. Was I being punk'd? Of course, Daniel said he was sworn to secrecy, but I operated under the old saying that three can keep a secret if two of them are dead.

I deliberated for a whole minute before throwing caution to the wind and calling her. She didn't answer, so I left her a message saying I'd love to hang out and to just let me know when would be a good day and time.

It wasn't too long before Rachel called back. Looking back, I must have sounded like a junior high kid as I hemmed and hawed, but I got across the basic message that I had a night off coming up—and would she like to go out for dinner?

"Uh, okay," she said. There was a pause on the phone. "But I'm bringing a friend with me. I hope that's okay with you."

This is ridiculous, I thought. *Why am I even doing this?*

"Sure," I found myself saying. And then I said we could meet at Santa Rita's, a local Mexican place, at seven o'clock.

We met at the appointed time, and even though there was a chaperone with us, we had a blast. I enjoyed getting to know her *and* her friend. But my focus was on Rachel, and I was pleased to learn that we had several things in common, starting with the fact that her father, Steve, had coached football and other sports at a Christian high school in Houston, Texas, before making a career change in the mid-1980s to law enforcement.

Her father had worked as a police officer in L.A.—he even

worked at Rose Bowl games—for six years until he suffered an on-duty injury when a drunk driver hit him. After receiving a medical retirement, he moved back into Christian education, making stops as a Christian school administrator in Las Vegas and in Orange County in Southern California. Then he became the executive director and principal of Vail Christian High School, near the ski resort of Vail, Colorado, where Rachel attended high school.

Like my mom, Rachel's mother, Liisa, was a schoolteacher, but she taught math. After Rachel and her younger brother, Joshua, came along, Liisa became a homemaker and a substitute teacher at their school. The last bit of information I learned was that she was nine months younger than me.

When we finished eating and had departed the restaurant, I leaned over and gave her a light hug. "That was great," I said. "If you want, maybe we can get together soon."

"Sure," she told me. "Just call me before I go back to Waco." Rachel had told me that her internship would be over at the end of the summer and that she'd be returning to Baylor, where she was a hurdler on the Baylor women's track team.

Our second date was with a group of friends, but the third was just the two of us. Because she was leaving Austin and returning to Waco, however, our relationship was kept from heating up too quickly. That forced us to focus on the friendship part of getting to know each other, which was a good thing in the long run.

After Rachel returned to Waco, we remained in contact by phone. During one of our many phone conversations, I suggested that she come to one of my home games in Austin, and she readily said yes. We zeroed in on the first home game of the season against Florida Atlantic.

Brad

Deborah and I found it very unusual that Colt asked us if Rachel could sit with us during one of his games. Colt had never made a request like that before. Debra asked Colt, "Just to be sure, you'd like us to sit with this girl at the game?" What my wife was really asking was, *Is she your girlfriend?*

"Yeah, Mom," he answered. "I've been seeing Rachel a little bit, so I hope that's okay."

Actually, it was *more* than okay. We were excited to meet Rachel, and we were immediately impressed with her. Debra and Rachel really hit it off, and I think my wife was thankful to have a little female company for a change at a football game.

Colt

After our game against Florida Atlantic was over—we won 52–10—Rachel stayed with my parents until I came out of the locker room, and then we all went to a restaurant together. Rachel drove back to Waco after dinner.

Rachel sat next to my parents for the rest of my home games that season, and you know how cameras love to find parents . . . and players' girlfriends. It wasn't long before speculation started about whether the attractive blond sitting next to my parents was my girlfriend—or my sister.

Sometime that fall, Rachel and I had our DTR—the "define the relationship" discussion. Before we went any further, I wanted her to know about my priorities, the things in my life that were important to me. The first of those things was my faith, followed by family, and after that came football. "But my faith is my most important thing," I said.

"It's mine, too," she agreed.

Then I directed the discussion toward the relationship part.

"There's something else I need to say," I began. "Yes, I have kissed girls, and I have done some things I'm not proud of, but I'm saving myself for marriage. I want you to know that before we ever get serious."

She thanked me for saying that, and then she pointed to the ring on the ring finger of her left hand. "My parents gave me this promise ring when I was thirteen and asked me to make a promise to the Lord to wait until marriage," she said. "I'm committed to this, too."

Attracted as I was to Rachel, at that point I knew it was a done deal—whether or not she realized it.

Over Christmas, Rachel came to my parents' house in Graham to meet the family, including Daddy Burl and GranJan. Of course everyone loved her.

Rachel had two semesters to go before she finished up at Baylor, and after she earned her degree in the summer of 2009, she moved to Austin and lived with a family whose daughters also went to Baylor. She took a marketing job with a startup web-based company.

I knew I wanted to marry Rachel, but I couldn't ask her just yet. I had one more season of Longhorn football to play. Rachel continued to sit with my parents at home games, which meant our relationship was pretty much out in the open.

But as the months passed by—we had been seeing each other for fifteen months—Rachel wanted to know where she stood with me. I'll never forget when we sat down toward the end of the 2009 season and talked about our future together.

We had already talked about our plans for after college, and she wanted to be clear that if the NFL was in my future, she wouldn't move in with me without being married. That was good information to know. I didn't want to lose her, and I told her so. Just wait until the season is over, I said, and I'll make things right.

First things first: I needed to ask her father for her hand. Rachel's parents had moved to Georgetown, twenty-five miles north of Austin, in May 2009 when Steve took the job of principal of Zion Lutheran School. When I met with him, he said, "Rachel has never spoken as highly about anybody or loved anybody as much as she loves you. I know she is ready to get married, and I know you all are talking about it. I want you to know that Liisa and I think you'll be great for her, so you certainly have our blessing."

It was kind of him to say that, and I thanked him. But I didn't tell him *when* I would propose to Rachel. The target date I had in mind was the Monday after the BCS Championship Game, which would be played on Thursday, January 7, 2010.

Next on my to-do list was buying her a ring. During the Christmas break, Rachel had gone home to her parents' home in Georgetown, while I remained in Austin practicing for the championship game against Alabama. I did not know much about diamond rings, but I had some ideas of what I wanted. One afternoon I dropped by Russell Korman Fine Jewelry in Austin and showed the woman behind the counter a picture I had drawn of the ring I wanted.

"Well, we've never made anything like that, but we can give it a try," she said.

How did I pay for this custom ring? For the last year, I had saved a little bit of money each month from my scholarship checks, which gave me enough to make a down payment. For the rest, I hit up Dad for a loan, which I told him I'd pay back when I signed a pro contract. (I have since made good on the loan.) I picked up that beautiful ring—it came out just as I envisioned it—just before the team left for Southern California.

After suffering the shoulder injury in Pasadena, I returned to

Austin. My plan all along was to ask Rachel to marry me back in Austin after the BCS game, but I had to do some scrambling because of my shoulder.

I wanted to see Dr. James Andrews, a renowned sports orthopedic surgeon in Birmingham, Alabama, right away. Dr. Andrews was well known in the football world for his medical expertise, especially on shoulders. He had performed shoulder surgery on Drew Brees, the New Orleans Saints quarterback, and on Sam Bradford.

I flew into Birmingham that Monday morning to see Dr. Andrews. Four days after the injury, I still didn't have any strength in my right arm, and the lack of pain seemed strange to me. After looking me over, Dr. Andrews declared that I had a serious nerve injury in my shoulder. It wouldn't require surgery, he said, but it would require extensive rehabilitation and strengthening of the muscles that affected the nerve.

After I learned where I stood physically, Dad and I drove to the Birmingham airport, where I called Rachel's father. "I want to give you a heads-up," I said. "I'm going to ask Rachel to marry me tonight, and I'd like you and Liisa to join us for dinner afterward at Santa Rita's."

My future father-in-law wished me the best of luck.

I needed some help because I had an elaborate plan for asking Rachel to marry me. At first I thought about taking her out to a fancy restaurant and having the diamond ring delivered after dinner on a plate covered by a silver dome. Then I entertained crazier ideas, like putting her through a scavenger hunt throughout Austin or hiring a horse-drawn carriage to take us out in the country.

But I remembered that Rachel had always said she wanted to go onto the Memorial Stadium field when nobody was there. "I'd really like to go out on that field someday," she repeated several times as we walked outside the stadium one time. "I'm always sitting in the stands watching you play, but I would like to know what it's like down there on the field when the stadium is empty."

Since Rachel knew I had to fly to Southern California the next day to begin rehabbing my shoulder, I came up with an elaborate plan: before we went out to dinner, I would tell her I needed to stop by the locker room and grab my cleats and some workout clothes. While we were at the stadium, the lights would be on, and Rachel would remind me how much she had always wanted to walk around on the football field and see it for herself.

That's when I would pop the question.

She walked right into my whole setup. As we made our way toward the stadium, she saw that the lights were on. "Colt, this would be a perfect time," she said. "Can we go out on the field?"

"I don't know if we can get in," I said, shaking my head.

"You have a key to the gate," she reminded me. "I know you can get us in there."

"Oh yeah," I said, playing dumb.

I unlocked the gate and escorted her onto the cushy FieldTurf. I glanced up and noticed the Longhorn logo on the huge LCD screen, which was kind of a screensaver for the Godzillatron when it wasn't in use.

I stopped at places on the field where I had scored a touchdown or had thrown a long TD pass and told her a story about each play. We slowly made our way toward midfield, moving away from the Godzillatron, which was at the south end of the stadium.

I had my arm around her when we reached the 50-yard line. Just then, a flash of light from the Godzillatron lit up the stadium seats around us. I released her, and when she turned around to see where all the light was coming from, she covered her mouth in shock.

There, on the stadium's high-def scoreboard screen, in big black letters against a white background, was the following message:

Rachel,
I love you!
Will you marry me?
Colt

When she turned around, I was on bended knee, presenting her with a small jewelry box with a ring inside. "Will you marry me?" I asked.

Rachel teared up and answered, "Yes, I will!"

We hugged and kissed. My plan had worked to perfection. John Bianco, the media relations guy at Texas, was in the press box that night working the Godzillatron, and I had a photographer hidden away in the stands, taking pictures.

Now the wedding plans could start in earnest. We knew we'd either have to elope or go big, and we chose the latter. We kept the wedding location—Westover Hills Church of Christ—as well as the date a secret, but there were 750 on our invitation list. The date we selected was Saturday, July 17, 2010.

We asked Matt Carter, the pastor at Austin Stone Community Church, to marry us, and that meant he would also be doing the premarital counseling. One of the questions he asked us during our discussions was whether we had remained sexually pure. We said yes.

Matt knew some of the struggles and temptations I'd had with women, and he also knew how important it was to me and Rachel that we remain pure prior to marriage. We had some great discussions, and he gave us some valuable advice for beginning our lifetime of physical intimacy together.

The wedding was a blast, and Jordan Shipley and country star Aaron Watson entertained the wedding party with a hilarious song called "When I Grow Up, I Want to Be Just Like Colt McCoy," which went directly to YouTube.

After we spent our wedding night at the Four Seasons in Austin, we flew out the next day to the Bahamas for three nights and two days at Harbour Island, which is famous for its pink sand beaches. We stayed at a honeymooners' cottage right on the beach, and sure enough, the sandy beach did have pink flecks mixed in. We mostly laid around the beach and snorkeled in the warm Caribbean waters, but Rachel knew how much I enjoy fishing, so we chartered a boat and fished one time.

I wanted to stay in the Bahamas for a week or two, but I had to get back to the United States so I could report to the Cleveland Browns training camp. We maximized our short time in the Bahamas by staying as long as we could at Harbour Island. On the morning of the third day in the Bahamas, we flew together to Cleveland, where I reported to camp that afternoon.

I promised Rachel that our second honeymoon would last a lot longer.

CHAPTER 15

MAKING HAY
WHILE THE SUN SHINES

Colt

Poor Rachel.

Not enough "Colt time" in the Bahamas, as she would later tell her friends.

Once we returned to the States, there was no reason for her to stay in Cleveland with me, so she flew on to Austin. The way things go in the NFL, you're basically sequestered at training camp for a month—no wives, no girlfriends, no family, no kids, no anything, not even for the veterans. For the next month, the Cleveland Browns owned me twenty-four hours a day. During that time, I would be either at the Browns Training Facility in Berea, a suburb of Cleveland, or at the team hotel.

Guys, can we talk man to man here? After three days and three nights of honeymooning, being separated from my new wife for a whole month was *tough*.

But let's keep moving. I signed my NFL contract within hours after our return from the Bahamas. The terms of the contract are a matter of public record: a four-year deal worth up to $5 million with a signing bonus of $750,000.

For someone who had lived on ramen noodles on more than a few nights in college, that was a lot of scratch. It was awesome.

But unlike the contracts in Major League Baseball or the National Basketball Association, contracts in the NFL are not guaranteed. If the team decides I'm not good enough to help it win, if I don't perform up to expectations, or if I suffer a career-ending injury, I will be cut from the team and will no longer be paid.

While I was grateful to sign my contract with the Browns, I couldn't help but think of how the 2010 NFL draft turned out. Before my injury at the Rose Bowl, NFL people were telling me I was being looked at as first-round draft material.

After my injury, though, my stock dropped considerably due to questions regarding my shoulder. I also heard the same old "concerns" about my height. Many NFL coaches and front office people are fixated on a quarterback's height, and they wondered if I was tall enough for the job. At 6 feet, 1½ inches tall, I was about a half inch shorter than the "prototype" NFL quarterback.

I would have argued that my intangibles tipped the scales in my favor. Nobody could say I wasn't a proven winner; I was the winningest quarterback in college football history, winning 45 games out of my 53 starts. Nobody could say I wasn't accurate; I completed better than 70 percent of my passes at Texas and set the single-season record for completion percentage with 76.7 percent. At my "Pro Day" in front of NFL scouts, I completed 55 of 55 pass attempts. And nobody could say I wasn't a leader; all they had to do was talk to my coaches, my teammates, and even my competition to get a bead on that. Or they could just watch some of my game tapes; they had four years' worth of last-minute drives and clutch third-down passes to choose from.

Nonetheless, as the 2010 NFL draft rolled around in late April, I wasn't on any of the draftniks' "boards" for the first two rounds. But I knew teams like St. Louis, Washington, Buffalo, and Cleveland were strongly interested in me because they had brought me in for private workouts.

I knew my fate was out of my hands. Since there was still a chance I might go early, Rachel and I, along with my parents, family, and close friends, gathered at the Anderson home—I was still living above their garage—for the first night of the NFL draft, which consists of the first two rounds and which was broadcast on ESPN. An ESPN reporter was with us that night to report throughout the evening while we waited for NFL Commissioner Roger Goodell to call my name.

I wasn't drafted in the first two rounds, so we all reassembled the following night at the Anderson home, each of us anxious about how far I had "dropped."

The difference between what a quarterback gets paid after being drafted in the first round versus what he's paid in the third round amounts to many millions of dollars. Here's one example of the difference: my buddy Sam Bradford was the No. 1 pick in the 2010 draft, and he signed with the St. Louis Rams for the richest contract in NFL history, a five-year $86 million deal with *$50 million* in guaranteed money. On the other hand, Tim Tebow, who most everyone agreed was the surprise of the 2010 draft when the Denver Broncos took him in the first round as the twenty-fifth pick, signed a five-year contract for $33 million (if all incentives are met), with $8.75 million guaranteed.

As far as I was concerned, all that was just more fuel for the fire.

I was still available as the third round progressed. Then, with the eighty-fourth pick, the Cincinnati Bengals picked one of my best friends—and the best man at my wedding—Jordan Shipley.

A minute after the Bengals called Jordan's name, my cell phone chirped. It was Mike Holmgren, president of the Cleveland Browns, who had the next pick. "Congratulations, Colt," he said. "Sometimes good things come to those who wait. We can't wait for you to get up here."

With jubilation sweeping through the Anderson veranda, something really cool happened: Commissioner Goodell strode to the microphone at Radio City Music Hall in New York and declared that Coach Mack Brown would announce the next draft choice, for the Cleveland Browns. Coach beamed as he leaned over the microphone and said, "With the eighty-fifth pick in the 2010 NFL draft, the Cleveland Browns select Colt McCoy, Texas."

It felt great to know where I was going. I jumped on a plane the next morning to fly to Cleveland to meet my coaches and team officials, as well as the media.

I had grown up watching Mike Holmgren when he was the head coach of the Green Bay Packers during their Super Bowl years in the 1990s, when one of my favorite players, Brett Favre, played for him. Coach Holmgren—everyone still called him "Coach," even though he wasn't on the field anymore—impressed me as a class act. He compared me to quarterbacks Joe Montana and Steve Young when they were coming out of college, which was quite a compliment, especially coming from him.

"You're my guy," Coach Holmgren said. "I'm going to develop you. But I've never had a rookie quarterback play for me before, so you're not going to play. I want you to watch and learn this year. Don't take a year off, but know that's what I want you to do."

That was the backdrop as I reported to camp with the rest of the Browns' rookies. Coming from a place, the University of Texas, where I didn't miss a start over four years and then hearing that there were no plans to play me was tough to swallow. I wanted to get out there on the field. I wanted to be the guy. Since that wasn't going to happen, however, I said to myself, *Okay, I'm going to be the starter in my mind.* In other words, I would prepare for the upcoming season like I *was* the starting quarterback.

The rookie hazing—a time-honored NFL tradition—started as soon as the veterans reported to camp a few days after the rookies and continued all season long. My head coach, Eric Mangini, made an announcement about hazing one evening. "We're not shaving heads or eyebrows, but besides that, you can do what you want," Coach said.

Thank goodness he issued that edict; I don't think Rachel would have appreciated me coming home without any hair.

I escaped a haircut, but the veterans constantly had me running errands:

Go to the store and get me some dip.

Take my playbook, rook.

Carry my pads to the field.

Get me another Gatorade.

Our starting quarterback was veteran Jake Delhomme, and the backup was Seneca Wallace, who'd been in the league nine years. I got to play in the opening preseason game at Green Bay, but I banged my thumb on a teammate's helmet on a pass and thought I had broken my thumb. The X-rays were negative, though, thank goodness.

Then, in our last preseason game, against the Chicago Bears, I had perfect 13 for 13 passing in a little more than two quarters of work. But I ended up in the locker room for X-rays because someone had stepped on my throwing hand. Again, I was fine.

Once the regular season started, I was the forgotten quarterback until the game against the Pittsburgh Steelers, when I got my first start and my teammates and coaches said I played well. I was aware I was on a short leash going into Pittsburgh, but in the back of my mind, I thought, *When I go in, I'm not coming back out.* That was my attitude, but since I wasn't the coach, I had no way of knowing if things would work out that way.

The Cleveland Browns had the toughest schedule in the NFL in 2010, and coming up after the Pittsburgh game were games against three more playoff-bound teams: New Orleans, New England, and New York. After my solid performance at Heinz Field, Coach

Mangini told me I would be starting against a Saints team that had won the Super Bowl the previous season. They had an awesome quarterback named Drew Brees.

I knew all about Drew and how he had suffered a career-threatening shoulder injury while playing for San Diego but had made a storybook comeback in post-Katrina New Orleans. Drew had grown up in Austin and played his high school football at Westlake High. He, too, had grown up hearing the "experts" declare that he wasn't tall enough to play quarterback in the NFL because he was six feet tall.

The same "experts" had said that about me, so I identified with Drew and hoped I could be as good as he was someday.

I met Drew for the first time at the Maxwell Football Club's annual awards banquet in Atlantic City, New Jersey, in March 2010, when I received the seventy-third Maxwell Award as College Player of the Year. Drew was also there in Atlantic City to pick up his award as the Bert Bell Professional Player of the Year after his Super Bowl victory, and I enjoyed being introduced to him.

In New Orleans, we surprised the football world by beating the Saints 30–17 in the Superdome. Our defense played magnificently, and I managed the game well, meaning I didn't do anything spectacular but also didn't let the Saints crowd rattle me. Meanwhile, Drew had a rough day at the office: four interceptions, including a pair of pick-sixes by David Bowens, one of our linebackers.

That day I finally got to catch a pass in a football game, just as I had diagrammed it many years before in church. After lining up in the shotgun, I handed off to our 240-pound running back, Peyton Hillis, who ran one way while I ran the other way. Then Peyton stopped and passed back across the field to me for a crucial first down. The 13-yard gadget play took valuable time off the clock and helped prevent a New Orleans comeback.

The big win in the Big Easy pumped us up for our next game, a home contest against quarterback Tom Brady and the New England Patriots. Practice was more fun that week, and our coaches were more upbeat. Many of our coaches had come from the Patriots organization, so there was an added incentive to prove something.

We proved that the win in New Orleans was no fluke by dismantling the Patriots 34–14 before a delirious sellout crowd at Cleveland Browns Stadium. "A shocker" was the media's favorite description. My favorite play took place in the third quarter when we were in the red zone on the New England 16-yard line. With no receivers open, I tucked the ball under my right arm and sprinted for the left corner of the end zone. I hit the pylon with a dive to score a touchdown, which put us up 24–7.

I was now 2–1 as a starter—against three of the best teams in the league—and I believed I was answering some of the questions about whether I could play "at the next level." At the same time, though, I knew how quickly this game can humble you, so as far as I was concerned, I was still playing week to week.

Our balloon of expectations was fully burst when the New York Jets rolled into Cleveland the following week. We played them tough, even after a couple of our starters on defense— Sheldon Brown and Scott Fujita—went down with injuries. I had fun directing a last-minute 59-yard drive to tie the game 20–20 at the end of regulation. It was my first two-minute drill in the NFL.

We were moving the ball in overtime, nearing field goal range for our kicker, Phil Dawson, when we lost a fumble. Then New York turned around and scored with 16 seconds to go in OT to beat us. It felt like the air went out of our 2010 season. I was injured against Jacksonville the next week and missed three games, but I came back and started the final three games of the season. Although I had a couple of "rookie games" along the way—meaning

I didn't play very well—I felt I did some good things. We were in position to possibly win most games until the end, but we finished the season with a 5–11 record, and Coach Mangini and his staff lost their jobs.

Two other things happened during the 2010 season that I'd like to mention. One is that our family had our own *127 Hours* moment. Daddy Burl was moving some large equipment with his tractor when one of the pieces of equipment hit him in the head and knocked him off his John Deere machine, which ran over his shoulders and neck.

By all rights, that alone should have killed him.

This accident occurred in one of his fields, and my seventy-seven-year-old grandfather was all alone, severely injured and fighting shock. When he came to, he looked up and saw the tractor moving on its own toward a stock tank. Then the tractor veered into a tree.

With a burst of adrenaline, Daddy Burl somehow pulled himself to his feet and trudged toward the tractor, which was lodged against the tree with its wheels spinning and smoking. When he finally reached the damaged tractor, he turned off the ignition.

Then he made his way down a hillside, holding his injured neck in his hands. Daddy Burl found a golf cart and drove himself toward my Uncle Michael, who was working on a bridge by the creek on the property. When my uncle heard Daddy Burl's whistle, he came running, got him into his pickup, and rushed him to the emergency room.

Daddy Burl had broken his sternum, some ribs, and some bones in his neck. During surgery to fuse the disks in his neck together, one of his vocal cords was inadvertently cut. My grandfather woke up barely able to speak. He can no longer sing and can barely talk, but he's getting better. We're now looking at ways to help him stimulate and regain the use of his paralyzed vocal cord through physical therapy.

I was in Cleveland when I heard about the injury, which was upsetting and made me appreciate even more that Daddy Burl is still with us.

I thought about how much I had learned from Daddy Burl and how much fun I had on his ranch growing up. I could spend all day exploring, chasing rabbits, fishing, and looking for arrowheads and "deer sheds." Deer often shed their antlers in Daddy Burl's fields, and sometimes those antlers can puncture a tractor tire. That would really infuriate my grandfather, so he offered to pay us grandkids a dollar for every point on a deer antler that we'd find in the fields—in other words, one eight-point deer antler was worth eight dollars. My brothers and I and my cousins loved collecting deer antlers for the rewards.

I've always loved thinking of all those happy times on Daddy Burl's ranch, but at the same time, thinking about them made the news of Daddy Burl's accident all the more disturbing.

The other noteworthy event took place during the Cleveland Browns' bye week, when the University of Texas team honored me in a way I had never expected by officially retiring my No. 12 jersey. The ceremony took place on Saturday, October 30, 2010, before the Texas-Baylor game.

Quite frankly, it shocked me that my jersey would be retired less than ten months after I had thrown my last pass as a Texas Longhorn in the BCS Championship Game against Alabama. When I walked onto the Memorial Stadium field, accompanied by Rachel, my parents, my brother Case (who was suited up to play for Texas), and Coach Mack Brown (my brother Chance couldn't be there because he was playing wide receiver that day for Hardin-Simmons, a small Christian college in Abilene), I was aware I was joining a very select group. Only Texas greats Earl Campbell, Bobby Layne, Tommy Nobis, Ricky Williams, and Vince Young had had their jerseys retired.

The public address announcer said nice things about me to the stadium crowd, and I received a standing ovation as Coach Brown and I held up a framed copy of my jersey for everyone to see. As highlights from my college career flashed on the big screen, I couldn't help but think of all the great moments I enjoyed wearing No. 12 for the University of Texas.

Looking back on that afternoon, I understand what a great honor it was for me to have my number retired, meaning that no Texas Longhorn will ever wear No. 12 again. They say it will be forever, which got me thinking—because forever is a long time.

In 1979 Earl Campbell became the first Longhorn to have his jersey retired, and in the three decades since then, UT has retired six numbers. If Texas continues to retire five or six jerseys every thirty years or so, then in a couple of hundred years, we could have three dozen numbers no longer available for the equipment manager to hand out.

Obviously, this could create a problem. Two hundred or three hundred years from now, when so many jerseys have been retired that they're running out of numbers for the players to wear, someone at the University of Texas might say, "Bobby Layne, Tommy Nobis, and Colt McCoy are names from the distant past that nobody knows or cares about anymore. We hereby decree that our players can now request their numbers because we need them to field a team."

Maybe that sounds improbable, but my point is that nothing on this earth, or in this life, truly is *forever*. Some college president or head football coach could very well come along sometime in the future and order that No. 12 be put back into circulation.

Neither I nor any other player from UT would have any control over what will happen after we're dead and presumably forgotten.

When you think about it, only one thing really is forever, and that is eternity. I made the decision to spend eternity with Jesus Christ when I was saved at a young age and became part of His eternal family.

You can make that decision, too.

When GranJan heard that Dad and I were writing this book, she said that as far as she was concerned, if we failed to point people toward eternity and God, then it would be a waste of our time.

GranJan was right.

During my junior year at Texas, an evangelistic organization called I Am Second contacted me about making a video in which I would talk about my faith and what was on my heart, which they would then post on YouTube and the I Am Second website so that people could watch and be impacted by my words.

Dozens and dozens of celebrities—athletes, coaches, musicians, authors, actors, and other people in the public eye—have made I Am Second videos. The producers seat each person on a gray chair with an intense light overhead that creates a dramatic black backdrop. With stark-sounding music in the background, the feel is intimate and personal.

This is part of what I said when the I Am Second film crew met me at my father's office at Graham High School and started recording my video:

> *What the world signifies as success involves winning, involves Heisman Trophies, involves All-Americans, involves lots of money getting paid, going to the NFL.*
> *For me, I am a success in life because I have Jesus Christ living inside me. I don't think God necessarily*

cares about wins and losses. I think He cares about what I am doing to make sure that I come and live in heaven with Him someday and whom am I bringing with me.

I feel like God has raised me, made me the man I am, and has put me where He wants me . . . playing quarterback. I want to win football games worse than anybody you know. I am a competitor, and I want to win. When I am on the field, the most important thing to me is what I can do to be the best and help my team win. And afterwards I know that I played that game for God.

Having a personal relationship with Christ is probably the biggest decision that any of us will make. It goes deeper than going to church or just acting like a Christian. If one of my teammates comes up to me and asks me, "Hey, man, how do I get to heaven?" I think that is a huge open-door opportunity to sit down and open up the Word and say, "Look, man, anybody can get to heaven. All you've got to do is have Christ living inside of you."

That is what I strive to get across to all my teammates: God is love, man, God is awesome. And He is there for you. You need Him right now more than any other time in your life. Because it's right now, it's not in the future, it's not in the past. It's right now. We are called to be followers of Christ.

I am definitely not perfect. I have my ups and downs. I make mistakes. Jesus Christ is the only man who is perfect in this world. He is the only man who will ever be perfect.

250 GROWING UP COLT

*So I don't want you to remember me as the guy
who made great plays on the football field, as the guy
who made great passes for a winning touchdown,
who made great drives at the end of the game. I want
you to remember me because I was here for you. I
want you to remember me because we sat down and
had Bible studies together and you came to know
Christ better.*

*When I think of Jesus Christ, I think of a warrior,
but I also think of a servant, and that is what I strive
to be.*

I am Colt McCoy, and I am second.

Even though I'm certain about where I will spend eternity, I know that my life here on earth is full of uncertainty. As I write these words, I know it's possible we might not be playing professional football in 2011, or that we may have a shortened season. There's much uncertainty in the air, but that seems to match the tenor of the times we're living in. That's another reason I keep my focus on the Lord, the only real constant in this thing called life.

As for my football future, if and when I get back on the field, I intend to make the most of my chance to play. There's a great verse in Proverbs 10:5 that says, "A wise youth makes hay while the sun shines, but what a shame to see a lad who sleeps away his hour of opportunity" (The Living Bible).

Making hay while the sun shines.

I like that.

We'll see what happens.

INFORMATION ON INVITING
COLT MCCOY
AND/OR
BRAD MCCOY
TO SPEAK AT YOUR EVENT

Colt McCoy and his father, Brad, are dynamic speakers who share from their hearts about courage, perseverance, and faith.

If you would like to invite Colt McCoy and/or Brad McCoy to speak at your event, please contact:

Sarah Dodds
The Flippen Group
4801 Woodway, Suite 300E
Houston, TX 77056
sarah.dodds@flippengroup.com
713-806-7227

ABOUT THE AUTHORS

Colt McCoy is the winningest quarterback in college history, winning 45 of his 53 starts during a storied four-year career at the University of Texas, from 2006 to 2009. He set numerous school records as well as the NCAA record for highest single-season completion percentage of 76.7 percent. He is the only quarterback in college football history to win at least ten games for four seasons.

Born September 5, 1986, Colt is oldest son of Brad and Debra McCoy. He grew up in several small towns in Texas and attended Jim Ned High School in Tuscola, Texas, where his father was the head football coach. Colt threw for nearly nine miles of passing yards and averaged more than three touchdown passes per game during a three-year high school varsity football career. Despite playing for a small Texas high school with an enrollment of 325 students, Colt was recruited by dozens of colleges around the country. He fulfilled a childhood dream by accepting a scholarship offer from the University of Texas.

Colt won the starting quarterback position at UT at the start of his redshirt freshman year in 2006 and never looked back. He won numerous awards and MVP trophies in bowl games during his four years of signal-calling at Texas; some of the biggest awards were the Walter Camp Award, the Johnny Unitas Golden Arm Award, the Davey O'Brien Award, and the Maxwell Award.

Following his college career at Texas, Colt was drafted in the third round of the 2010 National Football League draft by the Cleveland Browns and played in eight games during his rookie season.

Colt is married to Rachel, and the McCoys make their home in Austin, Texas, and live in Cleveland during the NFL season. He remains involved in the Austin community and is a spokesperson for Scott & White Hospital, which is building a children's hospital between Austin and Dallas.

Brad McCoy, the father of Colt McCoy, coached high school football and taught in public schools for twenty-seven years before leaving the coaching profession in 2010 to join the Flippen Group, a world leader in talent development and organizational performance strategies in the corporate, sports, and educational arenas.

As the athletic director of Flippen Sports, Brad works with athletes, coaches, and teams from the professional, collegiate, and high school levels. He has developed performance strategies and strategic plans that propel individuals and organizations to their highest level.

Born and raised in the Abilene area, Brad was a star athlete who played football at Abilene Christian University, where he met his future wife, Debra, who was playing on the ACU women's basketball team—which his father, Burl McCoy, coached. Following graduation, Brad started a high school coaching career in Lovington, New Mexico, but later returned to Texas, where he was the head coach and athletic director at high schools in San Saba, Kermit, Hamlin, Tuscola, and Graham.

Brad McCoy is known as a "coach's coach," and his new opportunity with the Flippen Group allows him to travel around the country to speak to coaches about how they can have a greater impact on the lives of their athletes.

The Flippen Group, based in College Station, Texas, has outlets in forty states and is the largest teacher-training organization in the country, also serving numerous Fortune 500 companies. The Flippen Group also works with several Major League Baseball and National Football League teams and individuals in player development.

Mike Yorkey is the author, co-author, or collaborator of more than seventy-five books, including *Playing with Purpose: Inside the Lives of the NFL's Top New Quarterbacks—Sam Bradford, Colt McCoy, and Tim Tebow*. He has worked with a variety of athletes from different sports to help them share their stories as well as their insights, and he is the co-author of the popular *Every Man's Battle* series, which has two million copies in print. He is also a novelist, having co-authored *The Swiss Courier* and *Chasing Mona Lisa* (to be released in January 2012) with Tricia Goyer.

Mike Yorkey lives in the San Diego area with Nicole, his wife of thirty-two years. The Yorkeys are the parents of two adult children. His website is www.mikeyorkey.com.